How to Open & Operate a
Financially Successful

Personal
Training
Business

With Companion CD-ROM

By John Peragine

How to Open & Operate a Financially Successful Personal Training Business — With Companion CD-ROM

Copyright © 2008 by Atlantic Publishing Group, Inc.
1405 SW 6th Ave. • Ocala, Florida 34471 • 800-814-1132 • 352-622-1875–Fax
Web site: www.atlantic-pub.com • E-mail: sales@atlantic-pub.com
SAN Number: 268-1250

ISBN-13: 978-1-60138-117-0   ISBN-10: 1-60138-117-4

Library of Congress Cataloging-in-Publication Data

Peragine, John N., 1970-
  How to open & operate a financially successful personal training business (with companion cd-rom) / by John N. Peragine.
      p. cm.
  Includes bibliographical references and index.
  ISBN-13: 978-1-60138-117-0 (alk. paper)
  ISBN-10: 1-60138-117-4 (alk. paper)
  1. Personal trainers--Handbooks, manuals, etc. 2. Personal trainers--Vocational guidance. 3. Personal trainers--Finance, Personal. 4. Physical fitness centers--Management--Handbooks, manuals, etc. I. Title.

GV428.7.P44 2008
796.06'9--dc22
                    2008015362

INTERIOR LAYOUT DESIGN: Vickie Taylor • vtaylor@atlantic-pub.com

Printed in the United States

Printed on Recycled Paper

Dedication

To my awesome wife and two of the best girls I could ever hope for. They keep me focused inspired.

We recently lost our beloved pet, Bear, who was not only our best and dearest friend, but also the "Vice President of Sunshine" here at Atlantic Publishing. He did not receive a salary but worked tirelessly 24 hours a day to please his parents. Bear was a rescue dog who turned around and showered myself, my wife Sherri, his grandparents Jean, Bob and Nancy, and every person and animal he met (maybe not rabbits) with friendship and love. He made a lot of people smile every day.

We wanted you to know that a portion of the profits of this book will be donated to the Humane Society of the United States.

–Douglas & Sherri Brown

THE HUMANE SOCIETY
OF THE UNITED STATES ©

The human-animal bond is as old as human history. We cherish our animal companions for their unconditional affection and acceptance. We feel a thrill when we glimpse wild creatures in their natural habitat or in our own backyard.

Unfortunately, the human-animal bond has, at times, been weakened. Humans have exploited some animal species to the point of extinction.

The Humane Society of the United States (HSUS) makes a difference in the lives of animals here at home and worldwide. The HSUS is dedicated to creating a world where our relationship with animals is guided by compassion. We seek a truly humane society in which animals are respected for their intrinsic value, and where the human-animal bond is strong.

Want to help animals? We have plenty of suggestions. Adopt a pet from a local shelter, join the Humane Society and be a part of our work to help companion animals and wildlife. You will be funding our educational, legislative, investigative, and outreach projects in the U.S. and across the globe.

Or perhaps you would like to make a memorial donation in honor of a pet, friend, or relative. You can through our Kindred Spirits program. And if you would like to contribute in a more structured way, our Planned Giving Office has suggestions about estate planning, annuities, and even gifts of stock that avoid capital gains taxes.

Maybe you have land that you would like to preserve as a lasting habitat for wildlife. Our Wildlife Land Trust can help you. Perhaps the land you want to share is a backyard — that is enough. Our Urban Wildlife Sanctuary Program will show you how to create a habitat for your wild neighbors.

So you see, it is easy to help animals. And the HSUS is here to help.

The Humane Society of the United States
2100 L Street NW
Washington, DC 20037
202-452-1100
www.hsus.org

Table of Contents

DEDICATION **3**

FOREWORD **13**

INTRODUCTION **19**

CHAPTER 1: ARE YOU PERSONAL TRAINING COMPATIBLE? **23**

Skills and Traits of an Effective Personal Trainer 28

The Personal Trainer's Tasks 34

Knowledge 36

Ten Reasons for Starting a Personal Training Business 47

The Business Plan...53

Business Plan Development 57

The Business Description......................................78

A Marketing Plan 79

Competition 80

Test Your Idea with a Business Plan.....................82

CHAPTER 2: LEARNING THE CRAFT 85

Apprenticeship 87

Online Training Programs 90

College/University Education.................................94

Other Training/Educational Opportunities.............98

CHAPTER 3: PLANNING YOUR APPROACH 101

Types of Business Relationships 101

Benefits as an Employee......................................102

Partnerships 104

Entry Points..105

Finding a Niche 105

Primary Research..109

Secondary Research 113

Competition 116

Fitness Trends and Technology 117

Entry Barriers...118

Exit Barriers...118

Developing a Marketing Plan 120

Integrating the Business Plan 125

Credentialing 136

CHAPTER 4: BUSINESS BASICS 101 141

What is in a Name? 141

Sole Proprietor 148

Partnerships 149

Incorporation 153

Basics of Incorporation..156

CHAPTER 5: BUSINESS BASICS 102 161

Operating Procedures...161

Evaluating Your Success after Six Months 162

How to do a SWOT Analysis..................................163

Surveys 169

Evaluating Your Success after One Year 172

Personnel 173

Management Summary 181

Personnel Plan 182

Insurance 182

Financial Information 183

End-of-Year Financial Analysis 184

How to Assess Success 188

CHAPTER 6: ADVANCED BUSINESS PRACTICES

CHAPTER 6: ADVANCED BUSINESS PRACTICES 191

Mission Statement 191

Pricing Services 193

Advertising Services 197

Location – Location – Location 198

IRS Forms and Issues 199

Business Permits and Licenses 200

What is a Federal ID Number? Do I Need One? 201

Self-Employment Tax 203

Tax Tip..203

Accounting Issues 203

independent Contractors 206

Confidentiality Issues..209

Desktop Programs that can Help...............................209

Is your Personal Training a Business or a Hobby?................210

Depreciation...212

Avoiding an Audit 214

When to Hire an Accountant 214

CHAPTER 7: MAKING YOUR BUSINESS AS SOLID AS YOUR BODY 217

Legal Forms 217

Insurance 219

Maintaining Records...225

Hiring and Firing 231

Payment and Collections 233

Cancellation 236

CHAPTER 8: WORKING WITH CLIENTS 239

Medical Review 240

APPENDIX A: CASE STUDIES................................. 241

APPENDIX B: WHAT SUPPLIES/FORMS
DO I NEED?.. 267

BIBLIOGRAPHY 273

AUTHOR BIOGRAPHY 275

GLOSSARY... 277

INDEX 287

Tip

The best way to get people into the habit of exercising is to slowly ease them into it. Set a routine for them that is fun and easy.

Foreword

By Matt Cole

Master of Science (Exercise Physiology)
Bachelor of Human Kinetics
Certified Strength & Conditioning Specialist
Registered Kinesiologist
Tel: 604.767.2034
mcole@peakexercisesciences.com

Have you ever been in the gym working out and looked over at the machine beside you and suppressed the urge to jump to your feet? You may see someone doing the wrong kind of exercise or doing it in such a way that you are afraid that they might hurt themselves. You may even overcome your reservations and talk to them and give them support. They smile and thank you for your help. A couple weeks later they may talk to you again about their progress and show you how much weight they have lost. They may even ask you for more pointers.

You have the knowledge and experience to be a personal trainer. You have been working out for years, you have built up your body, and you may even have a personal trainer of your own. You may be drawn to helping others build and sculpt their bodies in order to obtain the results that they are looking for. Maybe you felt satisfaction when someone smiled and thanked you for your assistance.

Don't let your hard work and experience go to waste – become a personal trainer. You can make good money doing something you truly love. Is that not everyone's dream component for a satisfied life? You may not know where to start. The great news is that you have already made a great choice. You have picked up this book and have begun reading it. If you are serious about becoming a great personal trainer, then *How to Open & Operate a Financially Successful Personal Training Business: With Companion CD-ROM* is a must read.

How to Open & Operate a Financially Successful Personal Training Business: With Companion CD-ROM is for the self starters. If you are content working at a gym six days a week for minimum wage, then you should not bother reading any further. If you are interested in earning five, or even six, figures a year while doing weight training, aerobics, and cardio exercises, then you need to take a time out, make a protein shake, and get a pencil and paper to start making notes.

Being a successful personal trainer is not just about knowing how to bulk up or slim down. There are so many other things to consider because it is a business. You may not know about taxes or liability insurance, but the information is contained in this all-inclusive volume. You can not afford to try to open up your own personal training business only to find out in a year that you owe thousands of dollars in back taxes. In addition, to help you cover all your financial bases, this book provides you with insider tips that can give you an edge over the competition.

You will learn about what sort of education is optimal to becoming a successful personal trainer. I only I wish I had *How to Open & Operate a Financially Successful Personal Training Business: With Companion CD-ROM* early on in my career. I would not have had to reinvent the wheel! Author John Peragine collaborated with successful personal trainers who have shared their experiences and advice for both novice and expert trainers alike. I have been in the fitness industry for many years and I can tell you that I found a lot of useful advice contained in this book that I plan to integrate into my own business. This is the information that they do not teach you in school, but that you do need to know in order to be successful in the fitness industry. Knowing the anatomy and physiology of the human body is very important, but so is knowing how to find a niche in the fitness industry and knowing how to legally protect myself should one of my clients get hurt during a training session.

John Peragine is a successful writer, with years of experience helping others realize and achieve their dreams. He has not only included forms that are essential to your small business, but he has also included a CD-ROM so that you can use the forms contained on the disc on your own computer. There are many forms and worksheets on this CD-ROM that give you tips and tools that can help you become the most successful personal coach that you can be. Turn the page and jump start your new career.

About Matt Cole:

Founder of Peak Exercise Sciences, Matt Cole holds a master's degree form the University of Victoria, specializing in exercise physiology and training methodology for strength and power athletes. He completed his bachelor of human kinetics at the University of British Columbia and is a certified strength and conditioning specialist through the National Strength & Conditioning Association (NSCA) and is a registered kinesiologist with the British Columbia Association of Kinesiologists (BCAK).

As an exercise physiologist, Mr. Cole has conducted research in the area of periodization and resistance training, overtraining, and taught exercise science courses at the university level. He has written academic papers on sport supplementation and doping, periodization, overtraining, and power development.

Mr. Cole's experience in designing and implementing conditioning programs is vast and includes the unique areas of fitness conditioning for the general public, active rehabilitation for soft tissue injuries, and sport conditioning for strength and power athletes.

Our philosophy is "optimal conditioning for optimal performance," with performance not only referring to the athlete's playing field or ice rink, but to everyone's leisure activities and quality of life. Optimal conditioning refers to how your conditioning program is orchestrated – individualized, structured, and progressive based on exercise science, sound training principles, and your measured performance and unique goals.

Locations:
Amazing Personal Training Studio – Kitsalino
World Gym – Yaletown
Spartacus – East Vancouver
Genesis Athletic Club – North Vancouver
Life Centre – Burnaby

*Read "How to Select a Personal Trainer" at **www.PeakExercise-Sciences.com** or e-mail me at mcole@peakexercisesciences.com.*

Tip

The reason people complain about their shoulders hurting when they do crunches is because they try to lift their upper body instead of their abdomen.

Introduction

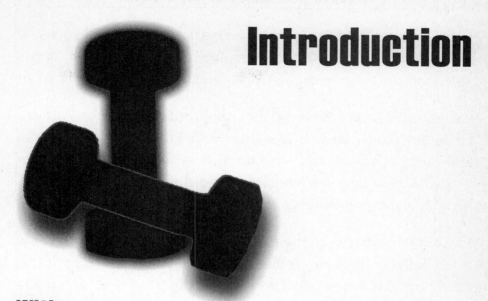

With millions of people eager to lose weight and get in shape, personal training is one of the fastest-growing careers in the health and fitness industry today. Fitness workers lead, instruct, and motivate individuals or groups in exercise activities, including cardiovascular exercise, strength training, and stretching. And they are well paid.

Until recently, fitness was considered merely a hobby or something rich people did in their spare time. Today, everyone is aware that personal fitness and physical well-being are intimately linked to longevity and the quality of one's life. Your physical well-being is also linked to your work performance and the joy you find in your family life. Personal trainers are at the forefront of this revolution in helping people to live life to its fullest.

Once the realm of amateur and professional athletes, fitness is now practiced by all ages and both sexes. Youth often wish to mold their bodies with exercise. Seniors exercise for health and to improve their general quality of life. Middle-aged people wish to avoid sickness, heart disease, and other ailments attributed to poor physical condition. Adequate exercise is seen as an inexpensive way of avoiding disease and premature death. Exercise makes us feel good, and we are capable of so much more.

Trainers work in commercial and nonprofit health clubs, country clubs, hospitals, universities, yoga and Pilates studios, resorts, and clients' homes. Increasingly, fitness workers are found in workplaces, where they organize and direct health and fitness programs for employees of all ages.

Individuals must work their exercise regimes into whatever time is available in their busy schedules. With the constraints of time, they must make the most of their stolen minutes. Personal trainers help them to make these available times count with expert advice, support, inspiration, and feedback. A trainer can help anyone attain a higher level of health in a remarkably short amount of time. Trainers help to bring about basic life style changes leading to better health over a lifetime. A personal trainer can help one become a greater person than he or she might have thought was possible.

The business of personal training is growing rapidly. According to the Bureau of Labor Statistics, personal training businesses are expected to become one of the fastest-growing business segments in the U. S. economy. There has never been a better time to start your personal trainer business and get a lead on the competition. You can begin to help people become healthier and happier.

Personal trainers are needed in a variety of settings, ranging from local gyms and country clubs to corporate offices and cruise ships. Wherever people need assistance working out, trainers are in demand. Personal trainers familiar with the huge variety of equipment currently used for fitness, and the equally large number of specialized exercise areas, are needed everywhere exercising is made available.

Where once, personal trainers only counted push-ups, sit-ups, and other repetitions, they have evolved into highly knowledgeable professionals in the areas of exercise, diet, strength training, and personal fitness. Today's personal trainers possess a global knowledge in healthy living, and they are trained to teach and spread their knowledge. They are well educated and have a desire to help others improve their bodies and their lives.

It is not enough to know what a body mass index is or what exercises will increase the size of someone's biceps. Personal training is a business. It involves knowing about finances, taxes, and insurance. To be successful as a personal trainer, you must be able to run a small business. This is true whether you are an independent trainer or the owner of a gym. This book will give you the skills that are often missed in even the best personal training education programs. In addition, this book contains a CD-ROM full of forms and templates that can be valuable to you as you begin and expand your personal trainer business.

In the first chapter, you can examine your own fitness for becoming a personal trainer, and start learning how to open and operate your own successful personal training business.

Tip

To gain size, the best repetition range is from 8 to 20. This is because the optimum result for muscle growth is lifting a size that is between 60 and 80 percent of what you can lift.

Are You Personal Training Compatible?

1

Suppose for a moment that you are a mid-level executive who has just joined a gym for help shedding a few unwanted pounds. You have just changed into your gym gear and taken two steps into the busy workout room. As you stand there observing all the strange machines with people busily slaving over them, you realize you need help because you have absolutely no idea where to start or what to do.

In various places around the large room, you observe several personal trainers assisting their "clients." One catches your eye immediately; he is bronzed and heavily muscled. That this young man knows how to work out is obvious from the muscles rippling under the skin. However, he also looks like the arrogant beach bully who kicked sand into your eyes last summer… more intimidating than a reassuring teacher.

Another trainer, a young woman, also bronzed and possessing a goddess-like form, is assisting a middle-aged man. Her fluid motions seem to infuse the area with a promise of great rewards if her client merely follows her instructions. You also see an older,

Jack LaLanne type. He is fit, muscular, and a serious taskmaster. It seems as though his drill sergeant-like demeanor will leave little room for mercy or forgiveness.

How do you choose between all the available personal trainers? The reality is that you will probably do as most potential personal trainer customers have done: You will march up to the front desk and ask for help. Alternatively, you will ask a friend, or perhaps a trusted coworker, to suggest a name. If the person you ask has any personal knowledge, or has been in a training program, he or she will provide you with a list of names from which to choose. These names will be chosen on the basis of reputation and experience. The most powerful sales tool that you as a professional personal trainer possess will be your reputation. Without this valuable possession, you might as well find a job digging a ditch with those bulging muscles.

No amount of knowledge, experience, or golden tanning will overcome a negative opinion of your personal training services. Many are attracted to personal training for the excellent opportunities, such as working on cruise ships, in country clubs, or at beautiful, upscale gyms. Those who prosper in the business do so because of their goals of helping others attain a higher plane of existence. They possess a keen business sense and know how to work with people in such a way that it sets them beyond their competition.

The powerful rewards intrinsic to assisting people in enjoying a healthful, nutritious life style, and the resulting physical fitness, are what retain those trainers who find value in other than monetary rewards. A job done well leads to a life enjoyed, and this, in turn, forms the powerful foundation for a well-deserved reputation for excellence.

The best fitness trainers love their jobs because of their ability to help clients live better, more enjoyable lives. These personal trainers derive satisfaction from a job well done, and their income will reflect this dedication and drive to provide a needed service. Successful trainers enjoy living the life style they teach, and they are focused outward in helping others to attain this feeling of fulfillment.

The popular misconception of personal trainers, as propagated on television, is that of selfish, narcissistic people who spend all of their waking hours looking at themselves in a mirror. These "beautiful people" seen on reality TV shows and elsewhere could not be further from the truth. While any individual who maintains a healthy life style will inherently be attractive to others, it is the dedication to help others that is the dominant trait in an effective personal trainer. Anyone can train to be fit; it takes a special kind of person to want to help others the way a good personal trainer does. It is a service industry that, while it pays a decent wage, is much more fulfilling in other ways.

The drive to succeed in assisting others, coupled with knowledge, skills, and ability (KSA), leads to success. This success creates and supports the reputation that is so invaluable to a personal trainer. We have now identified three facets to your success as a personal trainer: The look of a healthy, fit person practicing what you preach; a teacher possessing the knowledge to help others and the ability to pass on that knowledge; and, finally, the drive to succeed in helping others to transform their lives. There is a fourth facet that successful personal trainers know about: You must be a savvy businessperson.

Potential clients will probably not care that you are not a bronzed god or goddess. They would probably be intimidated by such people. These clients do care that you appear to be in fit shape, which indicates a basic inclination toward healthy living. If you do not care about your own health and well-being, why would you care about theirs? You, the teacher, must take care of yourself in order to be capable of caring for others. You are modeling for others what they should be doing in their own lives. You have to set the standard that will inspire others.

Let us look at what specific personal traits are found in successful personal trainers. The qualities that separate the effective trainers allow them to assist their clients successfully and thrive in the personal trainer business world. Start by asking yourself some difficult questions, which may require some deep, honest thinking on your part.

Do your personal characteristics match the needs of a personal trainer? Are you a patient teacher with boundless energy to deal with even the slowest learners? Are you a self-starter, capable of being on time for six to ten appointments every day? Does your knowledge give you the confidence to instruct clients in how to conduct their lives? Are you always seeking ways to improve your knowledge and skills? The more of these abilities you possess, the better your chances of success. Here is a self-test that you can take to see if you have the traits of a successful personal trainer. Answer each statement "true" or "false."

1. I like to help others.

2. I find enjoyment in teaching.

3. I do well under stress.

4. I am knowledgeable about fitness.

5. I do well talking to people in a crowd, such as a fitness class.

6. I am a flexible person.

7. I am there for the client and not there to show off.

8. I am a self-starter.

9. I know what a fair price is for personal training services.

10. I have contacts in the fitness and health industry.

11. I can make a business decision or a decision concerning what is best for a client and stick by it.

12. I can take a break when I need one.

13. I am a good listener.

14. I am athletic and fitness-minded.

15. I know diet and fitness dos and do nots.

16. I have enough business savvy to save money for dry spells.

17. I have a sense of humor.

18. I can choreograph aerobic workouts.

19. I can think ahead and make changes and adjustments when needed with a client.

20. I am cardiopulmonary resuscitation (CPR) and First Aid certified.

21. I can handle the emotional component that is involved with making life style changes.

SKILLS AND TRAITS OF AN EFFECTIVE PERSONAL TRAINER

No one person will possess all the skills that are valuable assets for a personal trainer. Trainers will have to work to hone the skills they possess and diligently attempt to find ways to make up for those beyond their current capacities. Some skills will need to be learned. Determination to continually seek success is one attribute you must possess to achieve the others. The learning process never stops. As you will learn in this book and by reading the case studies, continuing education and certification are important to staying on top of the trends in the fitness and personal trainer industry.

Additional characteristics that will allow you to thrive and grow as a trainer include an outgoing, friendly personality; excellent communication skills; good organizational and learning skills; and personal charisma. If you find yourself lacking in one or more of these, you should concentrate on improvement in that area. This book will help you hone some of these skills; in addition, it will help you with the details of running your own small business.

Flexibility in dealing with the various types of individuals you will encounter daily is an valuable virtue. Each client will have his or her own unique personality. They will also come into each session carrying the baggage of their everyday lives. Indeed, the release from work- or home-related stressors found in heavy exercise is often a driving reason for the client's attendance. One person may attend the session with the cheer of heavenly bliss, while the next may curse you due to a perplexing issue carried over from their work or home environment. You must be able to deal with each client as they come to you.

There will be difficult clients. These are the types who are wondering why their body is not chiseled after a few sessions. It may be easy to lose your temper with this type of client, but you must handle them delicately. You must remember that there is a distinct emotional component attached to body image. When people are unhappy with the way they look, they can become depressed and irritable. As they begin seeing results, they will come around.

You must have patience. You want to avoid negative publicity as much as possible. There may be times when knowing other personal trainers can come in handy. There are times when personality conflicts will not be resolved. It is always better to transfer problem clients to another trainer and part on good terms than to dump them and have them slander you around town. Every negative referral can take hundreds or even thousands of dollars out of your pocket.

The ability to maintain an inner calm will carry you through the ordeals of your daily encounters. Your clients seek your assistance in finding inner as well as outer fitness. You are not a mental health counselor, but your ability to calmly deal with your world as you find it will encourage clients in how they deal with their own conflicts. Good mental health is closely tied to good physical health.

You will need to be accountable. In upholding your end of the client/ trainer relationship, you will have no excuses for failing in your actions. If you are continually finding excuses for your behaviors, then you do not belong in this profession. Work hard to perform all duties and, when unable to do so, be truthful in owning up to mistakes. When mistakes happen, your good-faith efforts and honesty of the past will carry you past them. Many trainers draw up a contract with their clients. In these contracts, it is specified what the trainer expects from the client, but it also specifies what the responsibilities of the trainer are. If you are late or cancel appointments, you are not holding up your end of the contract. Your word is your bond. Do not squander it with empty promises.

Teaching involves a plenitude of skills. Foremost amongst these is the ability to motivate and involve your client in every activity during a session. Clients who are not motivated to succeed will not. As each client will have unique learning abilities, you will have to know each client and know how they are best able to learn.

To know each client's strengths and weaknesses, an effective trainer must have effective listening and observing skills. You will learn little about your client while you are talking. To learn your client's specific needs and how best to correct deficiencies, you must know that client and from what environment he or she is arriving into your care. This you achieve by listening and quietly observing. The client's words and body language are vital indications of how best to proceed with a training regime.

Leadership is another key skill in personal training. Effective leaders motivate by example. No one enjoys working with a trainer who sits off to the side of the activity, giving orders and chewing sunflower seeds. As a personal trainer, you should be with your client, assisting and working with each as if he or she is your only client. Positive reinforcement for each victory, no matter how small, will keep your client working even when you are absent.

The positive attitude you project to the world is contagious. Clients do not hire you because they find workouts easy. They are having problems motivating themselves to deal with their fitness issues. Leading them to better health with positive reinforcement for their efforts, even while you are suffering, is the sign of a true professional.

Motivating yourself is not always easy. It requires a deep self-awareness that allows you to understand your inner self. When serving the public, trainers do not have the luxury of being self-indulgent. Regularly exhibiting a positive attitude is another trait of the personal trainer. If you work at a gym, you may consider asking another trainer to barter services with you. That way, you are getting the benefit of someone motivating you while, at the same time, helping them.

A common mistake of new personal trainers is to be too competitive. There are usually plenty of clients to go around. Being on good terms with other trainers can enhance your services. There is much to learn from other personal trainers, and much you can teach them as well.

Each trait mentioned is not necessarily required to be a successful personal trainer. The more of these valuable skills you possess, the better equipped you will be to serve your clientele. For example, it will help smooth the road to an effective client/ trainer relationship if you are an inherently friendly person. But, through skills such as "mirroring," you can help the client relax and become familiar with you. Listening and carefully observing them will lead them to understand that they are important to you and their well-being is your sole focus.

The art of active listening is a very important technique to learn and refine. This is a process of making your clients feel like they are being heard. The main component of this technique is that you are listening to what they are saying without thinking about what you are going to say next. It is not possible to speak and listen at the same time. You have to seek to understand first, then you can seek to be understood.

If a client is speaking to you, you should try to rephrase what they are saying. This means repeating back to them what they have said in a slightly different way. This does two things: First, you are clarifying what they are saying so you can truly understand their point of view. In addition, you are making your clients feel like you care about them and what they are saying.

SIMPLE EXAMPLE

Client: "I am having trouble eating late at night. I am always raiding the refrigerator or looking for chocolate. This usually happens after 9 p.m."

Your rephrase: "So what I am hearing you say is that you have a late-night sweet tooth and you are looking for a solution to this?"

Client: "Exactly. I hate that I do not have the willpower to ignore these cravings. I feel really bad about it, but I cannot help myself."

Your rephrase: "So you want to be able to control your late-night cravings and feel better about your willpower. I believe I can help you with that."

In that last statement, you are rephrasing and opening up the discussion for you to talk about what you think can help the client.

Empathic listening as it is sometimes known, can really help your clients, and give them a sense that you really care about them and their situation.

Here are some other suggestions to help you develop your active listening skills:

1. Maintain eye contact. This does not mean to stare at them and make them feel uncomfortable. This means that when they are talking, you are looking at them. You can pick a spot just above their eyes on their forehead. This gives you the illusion that you are looking at them in the eye, but reduces the uncomfortable feeling that staring someone in the eye for any period of time can give.

2. Make sure that there are not any distractions when you are speaking to your client. Try to find a quiet place that has a minimum of activity and sound. Sometimes it is hard to give a client your undivided attention in the middle of a gym. You may need to find an office or step outside.

3. Pick a time to talk. Not all times are the best times to discuss certain subjects. Some clients can be sensitive about talking about their weight in front of the entire gym. Pick a time before or after a workout to talk about certain matters, such as progress and new workout routines.

4. Face the speaker when they are speaking. This may seem obvious, but if you have your back turned or are doing something else, this can convey that what your client is saying is not important. Stop what you are doing, face your body toward them, and lean in a little to let them know you are listening to what they have to say.

5. Let the client know that you are listening as they talk. You can say "uh huh," or "yes," or even, "I understand." This lets them know you are listening while helping you keep focused. When there is a break in their speaking, it is a good time to use rephrasing.

6. Try to keep your mind focused and quiet. This can be hard and can sometimes take work and meditation to achieve. When your mind is busy, it is hard to focus and concentrate on what the client may be saying to you. That is why rephrasing is important; it can help refocus you.

7. Try to reserve your judgments and keep an open mind. You may not always agree with clients, but try to listen and understand their point of view. If they feel like they are being heard, they will be much more receptive to what you have to say.

8. Be patient and wait until you are sure that the client has finished talking before you begin talking. This may be one of the hardest things to do, because most people will want to state their point of view rather than listen to the other person's view first. If you have truly listened to what the client has said, you will be better prepared to make a response that they can accept.

THE PERSONAL TRAINER'S TASKS

Your first task as a personal trainer is to get to know your new clients and evaluate their needs. You will need to understand what your clients' needs and desires are, such as to lose weight, tone their muscles, or be able to jog or run, along with some other overall fitness goals. These goals must be clearly identified through an agreement reached with your client.

Only after you are sure you understand your clients' goals will you be able to design an exercise plan with clearly stated steps that will accomplish their goals. A trainer should have basic knowledge of how the human anatomy works and how the body has to be maintained in order to properly design and implement the fitness plan.

Explain to the client how this plan will lead to the goals that you have jointly identified. Education of your client is a centerpiece of the training. If a client does not understand how a certain exercise fits into the overall plan, it can result in a failure to exert the effort necessary for that exercise to be effective. Their motivation will be lost because they may not see a particular exercise as important to shaping their body the way they want to.

You are the professional and expert, so it is up to you to explain how each exercise strengthens or defines a certain muscle group in their body. Through better understanding of the logic behind a certain exercise, a client will be motivated to undertake the more physically taxing exercises. The deeper the involvement of the client, the easier your job will be. Your ability to communicate ideas and concepts effectively will have a direct impact on the viability of your personal training practice.

As the plan is implemented, you will monitor and evaluate the outcome. If the plan is not working as desired, you must be able to adjust the plan to the needs of your client. All plans will evolve as one goal is attained and another takes its place. The constant work and feedback continues until each goal is attained. Once a goal has been reached, encourage the client to set even higher goals (and retain your assistance in attaining them). This is the basis for successful long-term relationships.

If you need to change a certain routine because it is not getting the desired results, you must handle it delicately. You do not want clients to feel it is their fault or they have failed in some way. You need to phrase your decision in such a way that it bolsters their confidence.

KNOWLEDGE

We have looked over the skill set required to be an effective personal trainer. We will now discuss how you acquire the information and expertise to work with clients to their advantage. There are two basic means of gaining the necessary knowledge and expertise: By going to some type of school, or by apprenticing with an experienced personal trainer capable of passing on their knowledge and experience.

Schools for personal trainers range from simple one- or two-day workshops to four-year degree programs from accredited universities. You must decide what your goals are as a trainer. Will you limit your work to helping out around a gym? If this is your desire, then gaining the basic knowledge required for certification will qualify you for such a job. Should you hold higher goals, such as running a successful service employing several personal trainers and perhaps a gym or two of your own, then perhaps you should consider a degree program. Specialized forms of exercise therapies require higher degrees as a prerequisite to certification and licensing.

Some states and communities may require you to hold a certain degree or certification in order to work as a personal trainer. You should do your research. Ask other personal trainers or contact your local county or state office that handles these matters and ask them. You can also check online or with personal fitness organizations.

There are many types of educational opportunities available for personal training. The various certification organizations offer basic education for entry-level certification. This entails about 500 hours of instruction and practical experience at a campus near you. You may opt for a junior college degree course or even for one of the four-year colleges. Your choice of degrees ranges upward through a doctoral degree. Of course, the higher the degree, the higher salary range you will be able to command, and the more specialized the services you can offer. There is the cost to consider and the time it will take you to obtain such a degree.

Accredited two- and four-year degree programs will not only impart the needed information about personal training, but also the ability to establish and run an entire enterprise. Consider investing the time and effort necessary to attaining a higher learning degree, which will open vistas not previously available to you. While certification as a personal trainer does not require successful completion of a degree program at this time, the knowledge and experience gained from successful completion of a program will greatly heighten your chances for success.

The more skills you have, the more expertise you can offer your clients. You might get away with a basic understanding of anatomy to get by as a personal trainer, but a degree program can offer you much more knowledge and training. Many college programs offer internships in which other experts established in the field can help you hone and improve your skills.

Certification programs are available from a variety of sources, depending on the type of training you wish to perform. Personal training jobs vary from working with individuals to improve their health and well-being to working with seniors, the physically challenged, the mentally ill, and with children. Some specialized occupations, such as rehabilitation, require a higher education degree program to enter.

Some of the certification institutions best-known in the United States include:

American Council on Exercise
www.acefitness.org

American College of Sports Medicine
www.acsm.org

National Strength and Conditioning Association
www.nsca-lift.org

National Academy of Sports Medicine
www.nasm.org

International Sports Sciences Association
www.issaonline.com

Aerobics and Fitness Association of America
www.afaa.com

As apparent from the names, each accrediting body has differing interests and goals. However, each will require you to exhibit a basic level of knowledge before a certification can be conferred upon you. You will be examined for your knowledge, skills, and ability (KSAs). They will provide (for a fee) materials with which to prepare for their examinations, along with courses designed to improve your own abilities and knowledge. Some of these organizations offer higher levels of certification. Once you attain an entry-level certification, this encourages you to keep studying, learning, and gaining expertise.

Constant improvement of your skills to accompany your ever-widening experiences provides your clientele with the best possible trainer. Not only are these improvements good for clients, but your practice and reputation will prosper under such a program. Your entry into practice as a personal trainer does not mark the end of your learning phase of life; it only marks the close of the initial basic level of knowledge acquisition.

The other course of learning is the entry into an apprenticeship program. If you are a promising and enterprising individual, you may be able to find employment with a seasoned personal trainer willing to teach you the trade. This is known as the "blood, sweat, and tears" educational approach. Through hard work and practical experience, you can learn from a professional all the practical aspects of the personal trainer profession.

One of the many benefits of being employed by another individual or organization is that you do not have to seek out clients. The employer markets your services and provides you with a client workload, and your liability insurance is paid by the employer. You will probably be working from a single location and all equipment and other service-related support will be furnished for you. Your employer may provide you with an employee benefits package. The package may be only payroll tax deductions, or might include a 401k investment and vacation, along with travel pay and various vacation options.

If you are apprenticed to a successful trainer, he or she will not only teach you the basic skills of fitness training, but also the business aspects of running an enterprise, should you desire to one day run you own business. There are many advantages to following the apprenticeship course. You will be learning from an experienced individual who has worked many years to glean his or her knowledge or the personal training field. What works and what does not work can be imparted to you from your mentor without weeks or months of trial and error attempts with your clients. Another telling point is that while you are apprenticed, you will be receiving a paycheck for your services. As a student in a school, you would have no income from your services.

Apprentices are expected to build their competence levels gradually in all aspects of being a personal trainer. Your mentor will lead you up the learning curve until you are capable of supporting your own practice. At that point, you will be able to make a decision as to whether or not you want to "go it alone."

The best possible option is a combination of formal education and apprenticeship. If you can get the education and, in the meantime, begin to work at a gym, you will be able to use the skills you learn while earning money and receiving the guidance of a veteran.

The business aspect of personal training is an often overlooked side of the profession. Any trainer not employed by a gym or another entity is self-employed. This brings another dimension to personal training. Being in the employ of another person or a company reduces many of the business-related cares and worries of being a trainer. You are able to focus on your clients' well-being. If you are a freelance personal trainer or have hired others to work with you, this book will help you fill in the gaps of the business side of personal training.

As a paid employee, you do not have to worry about taxes, insurance, liability insurance, operating expenses, and the myriad extraneous expenses inherent in owning a business. However, being an employee also places certain limits upon your horizons. In order to expand your services by hiring additional trainers, and taking on more clients, you will have to establish your own business enterprise.

The two possible alternatives to being an employee are being an independent (freelance) contractor and starting your own business. As an independent contractor, you will be responsible only for yourself. You will still be held accountable for your own tax payments, insurance coverage of all types, and all other aspects of self-employment, but your responsibility is only to yourself. On the other hand, there are many attractive benefits to freelancing.

A freelance trainer is able to establish an independent rate system. You will be able to charge what the market will bear, whether that is $40 per hour or $150. You will be able to work as many hours as you desire while making an equal or higher income compared to that of an employee. You will be accountable only to your clientele and to yourself. You will be able to set your own hours and be your own boss.

As an independent contractor, you would enjoy some tax advantages, such as deduction of applicable expenses. A tax accountant will be able to assist you in the complex world of small business taxation. A freelance personal trainer might find advantage in the many exotic locations available for providing services. Alternatively, you may wish to provide all your services from your own home gym. This independent contractor approach also offers the attractive feature of your ability to expand your business and hire additional trainers as clients are added to your workload.

One of the defining aspects of successful freelance personal trainers is their business sense. You will need to develop a business plan early on, figure out what your expenses will be, and stick to your budget. If you want to keep the lights on at home, you will need to learn how to market yourself, and when you get a little extra money, you will need to know how to save.

You can have the most chiseled body in the world and win many body-building competitions, but without a solid business sense, you will not survive very long. Included in this book and its accompanying CD is a business plan. This is a great template to work from to create your own business plan. It is a document that you will need to adjust as your business grows. It should be referred to on a regular basis and adjusted to meet your needs.

You have to be diligent about your expenses and fees. Stay on top of outstanding bills. Do not allow clients to talk you into cutting your prices. This is a business, so if you want to give people a break, you should consider doing personal training as a hobby rather than a full-time job. If you cut your rates in order to get more work, future clients will expect this cut rate as well. People talk, and most of your clients will come to you by word of mouth. Set a reasonable price and stick to it.

A successful personal trainer is organized. Look around you. If your life and workout space are a wreck, how do you expect to help others to be motivated and committed?

Successful personal trainers are calm and confident. They know their business and stay informed on current trends. They are professional at all times and always aim to please. If you are easily frustrated, personal training may not be your calling.

As a first step in deciding to establish a start-up business for attaining your personal training dreams, you should establish clear goals. Ask yourself if you are able to take on the task of establishing a new business enterprise. Are you willing to take on the burden of hiring and supervising employees or freelance contractors? Do you have the financial resources to support the new organization for the two years or more it will take your company to become financial viable? Will you be able to provide the time and energy to run this business?

Once you take the initial steps to opening your business and hiring employees, you have become responsible for the health and success of that business. Employees will not only look to you for work, but for that all-important paycheck. Once started, a new business takes on a life of its own. Depending on your leadership and decisions, it will either thrive or whither. Your new personal trainer business can become a source of immense pride or a weight dragging you down.

As part of the decision to establish your own business, you must return to the subject of your own personality. Many of the same characteristics that make you a good personal trainer will be needed in running your business. Being a self-starter, determined to succeed with the enthusiasm and organizational skills needed to maintain the business, is just as important to your new organization's well-being as it is to the physical well-being of your clients. Good communication skills, patience, and motivational abilities work for clients, employees, and others associated with your organization.

In order to be truly successful and make a living as a personal trainer, there are certain elements that you may want to consider:

- Do you have a willingness to take on acceptable risk? If you have an aversion to risk-taking, you will not be successful as a personal trainer.

- Do you have what is takes to take on a smart, measured amount of risk? There are people who left their high-paying corporate jobs to become personal trainers who are doing quite well. If you could take on a risky project, or one that you had autonomy in and were successful at, then you should do well as a personal trainer.

- Does the idea of sales intimidate you? Some people are not good at selling themselves or their service. If you feel you cannot be a good salesperson and are timid, you may not succeed as a personal trainer. You have to believe in yourself and be able to sell the idea that your service is necessary and that you are the best person for the job.

- Do you have the ability to delegate tasks? You have to be a strong leader and be able to assign certain tasks to others to get the job done. Without this skill, you might be overwhelmed and not be able to do everything that needs to be done. You have a schedule, and you must be able to lead others and tell them what to do without apprehension.

As long as you keep an eye on the business side of personal training, you can make a good living at it. You need to have reasonable expectations and a strong business sense. You have to devote time to marketing yourself because, while marketing may not pay money, it will generate money. You have to get your name and service out in the community. You cannot simply hang a shingle and expect people to begin knocking on your door immediately, begging you to train them.

Having a business background can help you make a living as a personal trainer. In addition to being able to negotiate contracts, collect money, and pay bills, there are personal business expenses and accounting that have to be taken care of. You have to know how to balance a checkbook, maintain an account, and pay your taxes to the Internal Revenue Service (IRS). Knowing how to develop a budget and pay your expenses can go a long way toward being successful as a fitness trainer.

Exactly what is your personal vision? Where do you wish to be in five, ten, or even twenty years? Is your greatest desire to be helping individuals attain their highest level of physical well-being? Perhaps you have a certain life style you wish to attain. Whatever this vision is, you must use it to define your personal goals. Once you have clearly worded your goals, you may start to shape your life and work to attain those goals.

Having someone to work with can be a beneficial prospect for you both. You can share in the costs of equipment, workspace, and marketing. In addition, if the other person specializes in training certain populations or has other special skills, such as being able to run an aerobics or karate class, the combination of the two of you can increase your client base and revenue. You can also help each other get the things done that one person may have difficulty doing. Depending on the type of agreement you come up with, this can also save you money, because you will not have to hire and subcontract for assistance.

The many practical aspects of establishing and maintaining a business enterprise will be covered in later chapters. It may be enlightening, at this point, to describe briefly the various business forms. The simplest form of an individual business is the sole proprietor. This business formation means that you are the sole owner and are totally responsible for all aspects of the business.

There are some considerations to make when taking on a partner. If you are starting a business with you as the sole owner, you would file what is called a "doing business as" (DBA). This is the process of securing the name of your business. You must understand that if you file as a sole proprietor, you are liable for losses, bankruptcy claims, legal actions, and more. As you are personally liable for these things, you could lose personal as well as business assets.

If you to have a partnership with another personal trainer, you have a couple of options. You can form a general partnership, which is less involved than forming a corporation. Each partner is responsible for what the other does, so it would not hurt to have an attorney draw up some partnership papers. They do not have to be legally filed, but it will help with possible problems and misunderstandings in the future.

If you are sure you have found the right person with whom to form a business, you might consider a limited liability company (LLC). An LLC creates a tax structure for a partnership and protects the owners from personal liability.

The other type of legal arrangement to consider entering with a partner is a corporation. This goes a step beyond an LLC in that it creates a separate entity from the owners. A corporation is an actual legal entity standing in and of its self. Under the law, a corporation is looked upon as an individual and is accountable as an individual. This helps to protect the owners from liability for the actions of the company, which they may not be able to control. Shares are extended as a proof of ownership to the "stakeholders" of the corporation. The total number and type of shares an individual owns determines the amount of ownership he or she holds in the business enterprise.

There are various types of corporations defined by law, ranging from a simple extension of the individual to complex organizations with many owners and the corporation itself holding numerous businesses ownerships. An attorney, or at least a certified public accountant, is best able to assist the business owner in deciding on the type of corporation to establish. The type of business organization generally progresses from the simplest sole ownership up to a more complex organization as the business grows.

Despite the complexities involved in starting and running your own business, there are numerous reasons to do so. Let us consider ten of the top reasons for opening your own personal trainer business in a pro and con format.

TEN REASONS FOR STARTING A PERSONAL TRAINING BUSINESS

1. Being Your Own Boss

Pro: This seems to be the number-one reason most people enter into business. They are tired of always having someone tell them what to do and how to do it. If you think you can do a better job of making a living, perhaps you are destined to lead your own company.

Con: Of course, this means there is no one higher in the organization and you must bear the responsibility for not only your actions, but also those of everyone in the company.

2. Personal Freedom

Pro: You are free to work the hours you wish, day or night, and you can choose your own clients and how you deal with them.

Con: You must please your clients in order to stay in business. If you have other employees, their well-being is of considerable importance to the success of the business. In fact, everyone with an interest in the company must be considered in all your thoughts and actions. This includes banks or other lending institutions.

3. Tax Advantages

Pro: There are some tax advantages to having your own business. Virtually all business-related expenses are deductible. You may be able to have considerably more income, with your business sheltering your gross income, than when employed by someone else.

Con: There is a heavy burden in keeping records of all types and being able to use them when tax-paying time rolls around. A business of any size will generally have to use a tax accountant to deal with the very complex federal income tax system.

4. Setting Free Your Creativity

Pro: How often have you thought you could perform a job much better than your employer? With your own company, you will be free to plan jobs and market in new ways that will be better than anything you were able to do while under the supervision of less creative thinkers.

Con: You will be bound by financial and time constraints. You could hire or contract outside help to tackle mundane jobs while you perform those tasks to which you are best suited . . . if you can afford to do so.

5. It Is Not That Hard to Do

Pro: Start-up of a sole proprietorship (you as the single owner/ employee) is not difficult. Tax issues are addressed as an individual, and all business expenses are treated nearly the same as an individual.

Con: The real problems and complex issues start when you decide to hire help.

6. More Family Time

Pro: You have the ability to spend more quality time with your children and spouse. This is true especially if you work in your own home.

Con: If you are a "driven" type personality — always working hard to succeed — then you are going to be dedicating a good deal of time and effort to the business. This is actually more of a personality issue than a business-related one. Businesses have a tendency to demand more and more time as they grow, and it is sometimes difficult to draw a line for your workday.

7. No More Coworker Issues

Pro: With your own business, other employees either will be compatible with you or will leave your employment.

Con: You could have a problem finding enough help to support your workload, but it will be you the workers must please. That is, unless you chase off all your clients because you are being finicky about with whom you work.

8. Choosing Your Clients

Pro: As your own boss, you can select those clients with whom you feel most comfortable. This will also produce better results for your clients.

Con: You will have to seek out enough new customers to keep your schedule full. If the compatibility problem is yours and you cannot find sufficient clients to make a living, you will have to face that fact and address the issue. If you find it necessary to terminate an employee, you must also consider the worker's client load and quickly replace those services.

9. Setting Your Own Goals and Deadlines

Pro: You will decide how many clients you wish to serve, not your money-seeking boss. Indeed, you will decide the size of your company and all other aspects of the business. You will decide where and when to deliver services.

Con: Again, you will have to please your clientele or face closure.

10. You Get to Keep All the Profits

Pro: You will not have to share any of the profits from your company. If you are an effective marketing and business manager, your business will likely thrive and the bottom-line profits will reward you.

Con: If your company does not make a profit, you will suffer greatly. However, if you were an employee, the bottom-line would always be the same on your paycheck, regardless of how well the company for which you work performs. Another issue with a business venture is that you will be forced into more of a managerial role, moving away from your original desire to provide personal trainer services.

It is obvious that for each positive aspect to owning your own business, there is an corresponding negative side. Your job is to weigh the pros and cons and decide whether it is worth the effort.

One less tangible issue in owning and running your own business is personal prestige. Most people respect and honor, to a degree, those who have proven that they are capable of successfully managing their own business. Our society holds such people in high esteem. This esteem is a byproduct of your success, and if it is important to you, you will work hard to achieve it.

Let us end this discussion with a self-test to review the material covered here, and to help you determine your own capabilities to establish a personal trainer business. Each of the following areas does not have to be your strong point. You should score yourself honestly and perhaps even seek out the opinion of family and friends.

The overall scoring of this test is more important than the individual questions. Areas in which you are strong will help carry you over in your weak areas. You should work to improve the weaker skills and abilities, while using your strong points to their best advantage.

Circle the appropriate numerical answer for each question. When you are done, add the total of all answers for your total score. After copying the test and having your family and friends score you, compare the scores and find those areas where they most disagree with you. You will likely score yourself harshly in some areas while "going a bit easy" in others. The overall score should accurately reflect your abilities.

DO YOU HAVE WHAT IT TAKES TO BE SUCCESSFUL?			
Question:	Cannot Handle It	Can Probably Do It	Am Great at This
Are you a self-starter?	1 2 3 4	5 6 7	8 9 10
The question is not whether you like to sleep in, but can you slap the alarm clock and sit up on the side of the bed smiling because you know you are going to love this day?			
Can you discipline yourself?	1 2 3 4	5 6 7	8 9 10
Will you be able to force yourself to do, not just the enjoyable tasks, but also the ones you hate?			
Maturity	1 2 3 4	5 6 7	8 9 10
Rate your maturity of approach to life, especially your dealings with other people.			
Personal Hygiene	1 2 3 4	5 6 7	8 9 10
Do you strive to always be "fresh and clean" in body and spirit?			
Patience	1 2 3 4	5 6 7	8 9 10
Do you have the patience to deal even-handedly with everyone, no matter how foul a mood they may be in?			
Knowledge	1 2 3 4	5 6 7	8 9 10
Do you have the knowledge for certification and can you adequately deal with every client's needs?			
Attitude	1 2 3 4	5 6 7	8 9 10

DO YOU HAVE WHAT IT TAKES TO BE SUCCESSFUL?			
Question:	Cannot Handle It	Can Probably Do It	Am Great at This
Do you always have a positive approach to the day and with everyone whom you come into contact?			
Determination	1 2 3 4	5 6 7	8 9 10
Do you have the drive to succeed, no matter what roadblocks may lie ahead of you?			
Personality	1 2 3 4	5 6 7	8 9 10
Do you have the friendly, outgoing, and trustworthy personality needed to deal with the public?			
Professional Character	1 2 3 4	5 6 7	8 9 10
Can you maintain the degree of professionalism needed to gain the trust and respect of your clients?			

Remember that the result of this test is a starting point. It highlights those areas where you need to improve. You likely knew the results prior to scoring yourself, but seeing the score written will make you much more aware of your shortfalls.

While identifying areas in which you need to work, you should also make the best possible use of your strong abilities. These are strengths you can use to make a success of your personal trainer business and your life.

THE BUSINESS PLAN

Without an accurate idea of where you are going and specifically how you plan to get there, you will eventually lose your way in the complicated world of modern capitalism and competition. Successful business owners have a clear vision of the products they intend to deliver to consumers and exactly how to make that delivery, while maintaining an equitable profit for their efforts.

A business plan is your personal roadmap to success. It is a plan for you to follow and one that will allow you to graphically illustrate the plan to others you wish to incorporate into your vision. Bankers will demand that you demonstrate a clear vision of your concepts, ideas, and concrete accomplishments prior to lending money to your enterprise. No one is going to entrust valuable resources to you if you do not know the road ahead. You will be defining not only what services your company will provide, but also excluding all those outside your particular area of operations.

While finding adequate funding for your new business is important, the person to whom a clearly written business plan will be of most value to is you. Your most important objectives, and specifically how to achieve those objectives, is your concrete foundation upon which to build the enterprise. Additionally, a business plan evolves over time.

As the business environment changes, the plan will need to be updated and altered to remain vital. As your customer base changes, or perhaps when you change locations or build a larger training facility, your plan should reflect how you anticipate making the most of these opportunities.

A good business plan states who you are, exactly what you wish to accomplish with your business, and how this company will accomplish those goals. You will include in the plan the assets you and the business possess (financials and experience), the services you will provide along with how you plan to deliver them (business operations), the specific consumer needs addressed by those services (the targeted market), and how you propose to perpetuate this delivery system (projected profit and loss).

Having covered many of the personal aspects of starting and running your business, it is now time to begin putting together the business concepts on paper. You will need a business plan to guide you and to help explain your concept to others, such as bankers or individuals who will refer clients to you. A good business plan will include sections describing the business, marketing plans, finances, and proposed management details. The broad format of the business plan and a brief description of each area are detailed below.

A business plan is a detailed description of all facets of your business. It is also a "living" document in that it changes along with the growth of your business. An excellent resource for you to utilize in working with a business plan is the U.S. Small Business Administration (SBA). The web address for all of the valuable resources at the SBA is **www.sba.gov**. This is a huge resource for virtually all aspects of starting and running your own business. Most information offered is free, and all has been proven useful.

Included in the array of information available on the SBA Web site are many forms and types of business plans. These resources and many more are available at **www.sba.gov/smallbusiness-planner/index.html**.

It takes more than just motivation and talent to have a financially successful personal trainer business. It also takes research and planning. Small mistakes in the beginning do not spell disaster; however, it can be difficult to get back on track and regain the advantage. If you take the needed time in the beginning to explore and evaluate your business and personal goals, you can use the information you gain to create a comprehensive, successful business plan that can help you achieve your goals more easily.

Developing a great business plan can force you to process and work through important issues that you may not have considered. The business plan you develop will become a powerful tool as you begin your personal trainer business.

The purpose of a business plan is to assist you in creating a roadmap that you will need to help you reach your business goals. A business plan also provides you with a way to track your progress as you begin and expand your consulting business.

When you set out on a trip, you usually begin by hopping in a car and driving. First, you need a destination. Then you need a roadmap to reach your destination. A successful and profitable personal trainer business is your destination. Your business plan becomes the roadmap to reach that destination. A business plan will keep you focused on your journey. It will show you where you are and how far you still need to go. If it is detailed and well thought out, it can also show you the obstacles ahead and ways around them.

Many moneylenders require a complete business plan before they will lend you money. This provides them with a look at the details of your business and, more important, whether you have included a way to pay them back. They want to know that your business is a viable one, and that you are a safe investment. If you have gaps in your plan or do not take the time necessary to create an outstanding business plan, they may not take the risk of lending the money you need to begin your venture. Here is a rundown of what a good business plan will do and why you need it:

𝚼 A business plan is an examination of your service.

𝚼 It shows what the market is and who your target audience is.

ϒ It creates a list of your competitors.

ϒ It shows your plan for marketing and sales.

ϒ It lists the costs of doing business.

ϒ If you will have other people working with or for you, your business plan contains a management plan.

ϒ It lists your finances. You have already begun the process of figuring out what things will cost and what your debt will be like. You will learn more about this throughout this chapter.

ϒ Your business plan must outline each activity in detail and include timing and constraints.

At this point in the development phase of your new business, you need a complete blueprint of the new operation — your roadmap to guide you to the ultimate success of owning a profitable organization.

BUSINESS PLAN DEVELOPMENT

These are the core issues to address with a business plan:

ϒ A description of your services and what needs that service fills.

ϒ A specific description of the consumer group you wish to serve.

ϒ How you will reach out to your potential clients.

ϒ How you will finance this operation.

You will learn about each section of the body of a business plan in this chapter. Contained on the CD-ROM is a sample Business Plan and a Business Plan Template you can use. Here are some of the items that should be included in your final business plan:

1. Cover Sheet

2. Executive Summary

3. Table of Contents

4. Body of the Business Plan

    4.1 Statement of Purpose

    4.2 Mission

    4.3 Keys to Success

5. Description of Business

    5.1 Company Ownership

    5.2 Current Situation

    5.3 Company Locations and Facilities

6. Services

7. Market Analysis Summary

    7.1 Market Segmentation

        Market Analysis (Pie)

        Market Analysis (Table)

7.2 Target Market Segment Strategy

Market Needs

7.3 Service Business Analysis

Competition and Buying Patterns

8. Strategy and Implementation Summary

8.1 Competitive Edge

8.2 Sales Strategy

Sales Forecast

Sales Monthly

Sales Yearly

9. Supporting Documents

Y Personal tax returns of principals for last three years

Y Financial statement (all banks have these forms)

Y For franchised businesses, a copy of franchise contract

Y Supporting documents provided by the franchisor

Y Copy of proposed lease or purchase agreement for building space

Y Copy of licenses and other legal documents

Y Copy of resumés of all principals

Y Copies of letters of intent from suppliers and others

Now that we have an outline, we will expand a bit upon it.

Cover Sheet

First, we create a simple cover sheet listing the name of the company, the owner (you), and complete contact information. This is where we see the importance of a good business name. If you have properly chosen a name, the cover page will go far in instituting a positive influence on potential readers of the plan.

Executive Summary

This section of your business plan may be the smallest, but do not underestimate its importance. It will summarize who you are, what your company does, where your company is going, and how you are going to get there. When you are trying to secure finances, you may have just a couple of minutes to grab the reader's attention. That is why this summary is so important. If it is not eye-catching and does not contain the necessary information, the investor may not read any further.

Your executive summary must be as thorough as possible, while being compelling, enticing the reader to continue. This summary must do the following:

Y Describe your company

Y Describe what a personal trainer does and what your personal training business offers

Y Describe market opportunities

All of this must be done in a concise and engaging manner.

Even though your executive summary will appear in the beginning of your business plan, you should create it last. You should write at least a paragraph to describe each section of your business plan. You should also end your executive summary with a breakdown of the amount of money required. Make sure that you list major advantages your company will have over the competition. One final item your summary should contain is a note that you have additional backup information. If you are planning to own your own gym, taking the time to create the best business plan possible will be necessary because you will likely be borrowing money to start.

A well-conceived, complete business plan will give the reader a snapshot of your business, your plans, and what you will need to make it all happen. You should include all your goals and hopes for your personal fitness business or fitness gym. Your executive summary will capture all of the important parts of your plan. Try not to make your summary too long or detailed; it should be a quick summary of the rest of the document. It is meant to grab the readers' attention and leave them wanting to read further. It should be no longer than two pages.

Table of Contents

The table of contents is obviously an inventory of the important points covered in the plan. Take care to list every major topic that a reader might desire to locate quickly. This will be undertaken after the plan's writing, unless you have computer software capable of compiling and updating your table of contents as you edit.

Body of the Business Plan

In the main body of the business plan is found a complete description of the business; marketing information; perhaps a description of your competition, employees, and administrative procedures; and any other information relating to the operation of the business.

Statement of Purpose

In this section, you will list all the major goals you have set for your personal trainer business. It should include the objectives you want to meet to achieve your goals.

Mission

The mission statement will be a statement of your company's mission or purpose. The statement goes further to answer the question of where you want to go and what you want your company to become. Be sure that your mission includes the health products or services your personal training business will be offering. You should describe where you want your company to be in three to five years. This will be covered in greater detail in Chapter 5.

Keys to Success

This area will contain your values statements. This is the set of beliefs and principles that guide your company's actions and decisions.

Description of Business

The company summary describes the purpose of your business using your mission statement and your keys to success. The company summary will identify your company's specific capabilities and resources. You can include a brief description of everything you bring to the fitness industry that is unique. This will include your management team, company organization, products and services, company operations, company history, and marketing potential.

Company Ownership

This section simply describes who the owners are and what type of company it is. It can even state what the plans for ownership are in the future.

Current Situation

The current situation section of your business plan should include key financial documents to support your projections. It is important that your financials and narrative mirror each other and work together. If these two parts do not match, it will send a red flag to any potential investors. You will be saying to your investors that you are either too optimistic about your sales, or you do not understand the numbers, both of which could potentially cause an investor to lose interest. Spend the needed time to create and describe your financial projections by using several standard financial statements. Once you have the numbers, back them up with your narrative. Any investor understands that these are merely estimates. What this does is provide them a glimpse of where you stand today and where you expect to be in the future.

Company Locations and Facilities

This section reviews your business location and operations. You will state whether you are a home-based business or have an office. You will discuss where your target clientele is and where you plan to work most of the time.

Services

This section describes the particular services that your personal trainer company will offer. Be as detailed and comprehensive as possible. Mention why your services are unique and better than the competition's.

In this section, provide the following:

1. A description of the services you offer. You should include all of your services.

2. What does your personal training services offer your clients that are unique?

3. What is the main reason people will use your service?

4. What niche does you particualr personal training service fill?

5. Who are your target clients?

6. What do your services offer that you benefit your clients?

7. What are the pros and cons of your services?

8. What particualr aspects of your services will attract your cleints to you rather than another personal trainer?

9. Where are you in the process of dveloping and creating your personal training business?

10. Are your prices competitive in the fitness market?

11. What aspect of your service is your main selling point to potential clients?

12. What is your personal training service length of service? What is the average time that a client utilitize your services?

Market Analysis Summary

In this section, you will discuss the market analysis by determining and defining the characteristics of the market you will be targeting for sales and the measurement of that market's capacity to buy your services. This analysis will identify and quantify the customers you will be targeting for sales. You will need to understand the strength and size of the market in which you will be competing. The analysis of your competition will help you better formulate and shape your plans. Be sure you can verify every finding that you have contained in your market analysis summary. This verification will come from articles in magazines, trade publications, newspapers, book references, research data, and customer surveys. If you have an outside agency do your analysis, be sure to refer to the report and attach it to your business plan.

To assist you in your market analysis, you can use the following worksheet. It is divided into three levels of markets. These are the different areas from which you are considering drawing for clients. An example is primary market — local gym, secondary market — health food stores, tertiary market — weight loss groups.

SAMPLE MARKET ANALYSIS			
Market Analysis	Primary Market	Secondary Market	Tertiary Market
What is the total size of your targeted fitness market?			

SAMPLE MARKET ANALYSIS			
Market Analysis	Primary Market	Secondary Market	Tertiary Market
Local			
Regional			
What are the historical, current, and future (assumed) growth rates of the fitness industry? Historical Current Future			
What changing needs do you see in the future use of personal training?			
Are there any fitness industry studies or statistics that you can cite?			
Describe any recent fitness training industry and personal training industry developments.			
List any identifiable market niches for personal training.			
What are, or will be, your customer's needs and desires for their health and fitness?			
Are there any common attributes that your clients in your identified market have in common?			
What is your plan for attracting and finding clients?			
What kind of advertising is your target market responsive to?			
What do existing customers like about your fitness training service?			
Who else has a need for the service you supply?			

SAMPLE MARKET ANALYSIS			
Market Analysis	Primary Market	Secondary Market	Tertiary Market
Will you be offering the type of service that people who want to improve their fitness, health and body shape will buy?			
Are your target markets clients, businesses, or both?			

Market Segmentation

This section of the business plan will describe the subset of prospects that is most likely to purchase your service. If this section is done properly, it will help to ensure the highest return for your marketing and sales expenditures. Depending on whether you are selling your services to individual consumers or to particular businesses, such as fitness gyms, there are definite differences in what you will consider when defining market segments.

We will assume that your market is local or regional. Let us suppose that you reside in a community of about 25,000 people. You will need to figure out the demographics of your particular community. Then you will break them up into segments. Here is a sample:

Y Age: 20s, 30s, 40s, 50s, seniors

Y Gender: male, female

Y Education: graduated high school, bachelor's degree, postgraduate degree

Y Income: low, middle, high

Y Marital status: single, married, engaged

Y Ethnic background

Y Religious background

You can locate this information through the newspaper, local town hall, library, or local chamber of commerce.

You will then break up and segment the market using psychographics:

Psychographics are attributes relating to personality, values, attitudes, interests, or life styles. These are also referred to as IAO variables (for interests, attitudes, and opinions).

Y Social class: low, middle, high

Y Life style: conservative, trendy, risk-taking, sporty

Y Interests: sports, shopping, reading, movies

Y Attitudes: environmentally minded, conservationist

You may want to figure out their buying patterns, such as whether they buy locally, in bulk, on sale, or seasonally. You should have a good idea who your target client will be. You could even include a description of your target client:

"My target client is the 27- to 29-year-old middle-class woman looking to tone her body and return to the clothes size she wore in high school."

If you are on the ball, you might even know the current number of eligible women who could use your service in your area.

Knowing this number can direct your marketing and let your investors know how much potential revenue you can expect.

There may be many people working out in a gym every day who do not know about your personal training services. Each of those people is a potential client. They may have heard about your service, but may not know the difference between your personal training services and other trainers offering similar services. This means that you have your job cut out for you. You have to target this group in order to let them know who you are and why they cannot live without you.

For example, if you want to extend your target group to men ages 21 to 32, you must find ways to communicate with this age group, thereby creating a bigger, more profitable market.

You may also find in your research that your target audience is too small and that out of a population of 25,000, only 100 people fall into your target area of 27- to 29-year-olds. If these hundred people are rich and will pay any price for your service, you have nothing to fear. If, on the other hand, they are low or lower middle-class, you may have to start your process over again. You may want to widen your market and redefine the services you will offer as a personal trainer or where you plan to offer your services.

Market Analysis (Pie Chart and Table)

The following pie chart and table break down your market segments and create a visual representation. Some investors like to see what you are talking about. You have to balance the number of charts and graphs in your business plan, but the right amount can look professional and can provide just the edge you need.

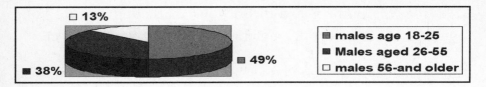

MARKET ANALYSIS							
		2003	2004	2005	2006	2007	
Potential Customers	Growth						CAGR
Males 18–25	5%	1,500	1,575	1,654	1,737	1,824	5.01%
Males 26–55	5%	5,000	5,250	5,513	5,789	6,078	5.00%
Males 56+	5%	1,000	1,050	1,103	1,158	1,216	5.01%
Total	5%	7,500	7,875	8,270	8,684	9,118	5.00%

* CAGR — Compound Annual Growth Rate is the year-over-year growth rate for an investment for a specified period of time. The compound annual growth rate is calculated by taking the nth root of the total percentage growth rate, where n is the number of years in the period being considered.

$$CAGR = \left(\frac{\text{Ending Value}}{\text{Beginning Value}} \right)^{(1 \div \text{\# of years})} - 1$$

Target Market Segment Strategy

In this section, you will write out what your strategy will be for accessing your target audience. This can include occasions such health fairs, free consultations at a gym, blood drives, and educational events. It can include placing flyers and business cards in places where clients are likely to see them, such as gyms, schools, and health food stores. Once you gain the attention of the target market, you will write out your plan for securing their business and future business prospects. Ideas included in this section can be competitive prices, package deals, and flexible finance deals.

Market Needs

The fitness industry has a need for more personal trainers as the number of people trying to get fit and needing motivation is on the rise. This creates a niche in the larger industry. Finding a niche in the market is the key to success. You will also describe why a person would choose to use a personal trainer. In this section, you will describe the holes that need to be filled in the fitness industry. This is important to help you focus your business, and anyone willing to finance your venture will want to know why they should loan you money and that the business you have chosen to build is lucrative.

Service Business Analysis

In this section, you should consider how your business is a cut above the rest. Explain what services you will offer that will attract clients. Analyze each item or service point by point. This can be an important exercise to sculpt your business into something unique.

Competition and Buying Patterns

In this section, you will analyze your competition: determine who they are, where they are, and what they offer. Try to be as thorough as possible. This list will be important to you in years to come, as it will be added to and edited. It is something that a person looking at your business plan will want to see. Having a good idea of who your competition is and what they have to offer can help you decide whether the marketing area is flooded with personal trainers or is lacking. Keeping an up-to-date list of competitors gives you the edge of knowing if your services and prices are competitive enough to keep your company afloat. Look at the Web sites and materials that your competition offers and study them closely. Do they provide number of clients? Do they provide the cost of their services? What seems to be their target market?

Strategy and Implementation Summary

This section will contain your marketing strategy and how you plan to implement it. Specify if you will have a Web site, if you will have a professional logo created, and what other kinds of business and marketing materials you will have created. You should also describe how you will distribute these materials so they get to your target market. This is just a summary and should be clear and to the point.

Competitive Edge

Explain what gives your company the competitive edge over the competition, whether it is your experience, your relationship with local gyms, your education, or something as simple as your easygoing personality or your physique. This needs to be a list of the things that your competitors wish they had.

Sales Strategy

Determine where you plan to advertise your business, whether it will be in the papers, magazines, or on the Internet. How much will this cost? The next step is to calculate your sales revenue for a year. If you follow some of the suggestions in this book concerning giving out business cards and conducting surveys, you will have a clearer understanding of how your advertising is affecting your sales.

You can make some forecasts on the number of sales based upon your past performance. This helps you to create a budget and know when to put your advertising into high gear, should your projections begin to slip. You can also track to whom you are selling your services the most, whether it is to men or women, a particular age group, or a particular type of person. This helps you direct your marketing to the group you are selling to the most.

There will be more components to your business plan described later. The components listed above are recommended for beginning your business. As you grow, add employees, and review your business's progress and viability, you will be adding sections, information, and data to your business plan.

SALES FORECAST			
Sales	FY 2007	FY 2008	FY 2009
Males 18 – 25	$54,200	$65,030	$71,544
Males 26 – 55	$25,800	$30,960	$34,056
Males 56+	$15,300	$18,360	$20,196
Total Sales	$95,300	$114,360	$125,796
Direct Cost of Sales	FY 2007	FY 2008	FY 209
Row 1	$0	$0	$0
Row 1	$0	$0	$0
Other	$0	$0	$0
Subtotal Direct Cost of Sales	$0	$0	$0

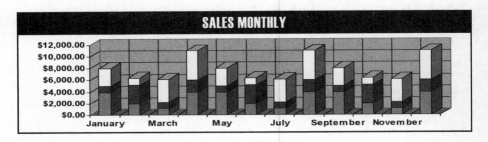

SALES MONTHLY

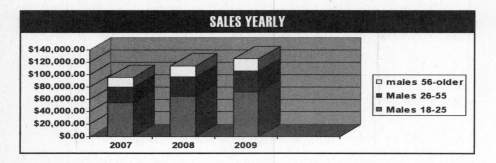

SUGGESTIONS ON BUSINESS PLAN WRITING

Writing a great business plan can be a difficult task. Here is a list of suggestions that can make the task a little easier to manage:

1. Do not try to complete the entire plan at once. Do it in small sessions and try to write a little at a time. Once you have some ideas written down, find someone who can read objectively and give their honest opinion and guidance. This does not have to be a businessperson and, in some situations, it may be better if it is not. This person can give a fresh, unbiased opinion that may prove to be helpful in your quest to write the best plan possible.

2. Let all your ideas flow naturally. Do not worry about the format until you are ready to put it in the final draft. Being too concerned with format can take away from the creative process. You must be able to capture the essence and passion of your personal trainer business while including all of the financial and technical pieces as well.

   You must have accurate financial information, and you have to make the numbers work. This is a fine balancing act. You must move the reader with your passion and your financial sense in order to get financial backing.

3. Include charts, tables, and graphs to present and analyze information. Visual presentation of your numbers can really grab someone's attention, and it can help them understand the facts and figures you are presenting.

4. It is essential that you include certain key components in your business plan. In your goals and mission statement section, develop realistic strategies to meet those goals. You are giving a vision of the way your business is now and what you project it will be like in the future.

SUGGESTIONS ON BUSINESS PLAN WRITING

- To make your mission statement stand out, consider adding and explanation of why you have chosen to create your personal trainer business. Your vision and values statements should be clear and concise.

- Your goals statement should capture what you plan to do with your business and how you plan to achieve it. The goals you create are clearer when they are time-based and measurable. They must be achievable, and you must have the numbers and research to support them.

- Be clear when you lay out strategies that you intend to use to achieve your goals. You should also include who will be responsible for achieving the goals you have created. Your strategies may include more than one goal, or one goal may have a number of strategies.

5. If you plan to have a partnership or create a company, you may want to consider using a well-connected team. If investors know people with whom you are working or who are on your board, you have a better chance of securing financial backing for your personal trainer business. If you are a sole proprietor, you may want to get letters of support and recommendation to help you on your way.

6. Keep press clippings. If there are any items in media form, such as newspaper or magazines articles, about you or your business, be sure to save them. It is a good idea to get some public relations started, such as publishing an article or doing an interview in a fitness industry media venue, or even local media outlets.

7. Keep your plan professional. Stick to the facts and always base your statements on the facts you present. Do not use generalizations or statements like, "My business will be a grand success." Investors want to hear about numbers and facts. They will create their own opinions about the potential of your personal trainer business.

8. In addition to keeping your plan fact-based, keep it lean. Do not try to fluff it up with too much detail. Make it clear, concise, and to the point. If it is too long, people will only skim it and will not be very interested in your plan. If it is interesting and a quick read, you are more likely to get a positive response.

SUGGESTIONS ON BUSINESS PLAN WRITING

9. If you have others working with you, or even vendors with whom you will be working exclusively, involve them in the creation of your business plan and include what they have to offer and what they will add to your business. Have your key people involved in the process. Not only will it create a better plan, but it can work out other business-related concerns as well. If you have everyone involved, they will have more invested into the business and its goals.

10. Make sure you are reviewing your plan at least annually, if not more often. This is not just a review of the budget and finances. You should review your goal and vision statement to see if it still fits. In addition, as your business grows, you need to make sure that your business plan and the goals of the company grow with it. If you only review the numbers, you may miss the opportunity to grow and flourish. You need to review where you have been, where you are, and where you intend to go. This will keep you on track. Personal trainer businesses that only focus on the budget and numbers often fail to stay in business over the long-term.

11. Your business plan can help you improve your overall job and business performance. If you have partners or vendors with whom you regularly work, try to meet with them about once a month. Review performance and how the business plan is going. Review the numbers and see whether you are staying within your projected budget, and review any new competition that may have arisen.

12. Look for a mentor: someone who has experience in small business or the fitness industry who believes in you and your company. He or she can offer you advice and support when needed to make sound business decisions, help you with your business plan, and be there when your personal trainer business has its inevitable difficulties.

13. If you live near a university with a master's of business administration (MBA) program, you may be presented with a unique opportunity. Many MBA students must create a complete business plan as part of their program. You can send your business plan to be reviewed by an MBA and get suggestions on how to improve it. This professional help is free, and the students are motivated to get it right.

14. Make friends with vendors and other small business owners. Join a chamber of commerce or similar business group. Do not be afraid to ask other people questions. You can offer your services as a personal trainer; in return, you can ask them to help you in your business with their own knowledge and expertise.

SUGGESTIONS ON BUSINESS PLAN WRITING

15. Try to locate a university-affiliated small business development center. These are great resources, as they often offer free advice and free or inexpensive workshops to small business owners. They provide resources and information regarding every business aspect of your personal trainer business. Find such services as one-day seminars on getting your business started, free one-on-one counseling, clinics on the legal aspects of your business, online resources, and downloadable forms.

EXECUTIVE SUMMARY WORKSHEET

Business Plan of (Name of your Personal Trainer Business)

_____

The purpose of the company is to provide personal trainer services. (If you want to list the particular services that your business will offer, list them here.)

_____

The mission statement of (company name) is _____

_____.

The long-term goals of (company name) are to _____

_____.

Market Analysis

The annual gross sales of the personal trainer industry are approximately
$ _____

Service Analysis

The service that (company name) will provide is personal training (you can be more specific if you wish)._____

_____

(Company name) will be unique in the personal trainer industry because _____

_____

_____

EXECUTIVE SUMMARY WORKSHEET

Business Operations (Company name) will be operated by (names of the owners):_____

Management of the Company

The company will be managed by _____
(This can be different than the owners in certain situations.)

The desired qualifications of the key management personnel are _____
_____
(Fill this in if you have other people working with you. Ignore it if you have sole proprietorship.)

Market Strategy

The target market for this service is _____

The marketing plan for (company name) is _____

Financial Plans

(Company name) annual revenue projections are _____

(Company name) immediate and long-term financing needs are _____

THE BUSINESS DESCRIPTION

This is simply a brief description of the services you provide. As you will be providing a limited type of service, at least in the starting phase of the business, do not make broad, sweeping statements, such as, "We are a full-service training facility." Instead, attempt to be specific, such as, "We specialize in weight reduction techniques targeted for individuals with obesity issues." The latter provides a much better idea of your exact services.

A MARKETING PLAN

This section describes how you will reach out into the community and get your clients. There are a multitude of possible techniques and technologies available, ranging from word of mouth to newspaper advertisements and radio advertisements. First, identify your target market, as in the above business description of obesity services.

Knowing and understanding your potential market allows you to plan your marketing adventure. Where would be the best location to catch the eye or ear of overweight people? Perhaps the best locations are where food is found — especially food leading to obesity. Fast-food joints, grocery stores, and those huge buffet restaurants are ideal locations for targeting large populations of overweight people. Most of these establishments have a provision for placing flyers or posters advertising your services.

Another location to advertise subtly is an over-eater club. These Individuals here have already made a decision toward, and perhaps a commitment to, weight loss. You could volunteer to provide some lower-level exercises for no charge and would likely pick up paying clients as a result. Considering that you will be charged for most forms of advertising, a donation of your time is an excellent investment and will probably return a higher rate than printed words on a page. In addition, it will allow you to form bonds with these people quickly and they can "spread the word" about this "great trainer" they met who helped them to shed unwanted pounds.

The whole point of market planning is to find where you can reach your potential clients and creatively develop ways to get them to come to you for services. This is one area of your business where you will expend valuable resources in hopes of attracting new resources in return. As a personal trainer business involves attracting only enough clients to fill your personal training schedule, at least in the beginning, your output for marketing should be fairly limited. Sometimes, simple word-of-mouth advertising will attract a sufficient number of new clients to keep you at near full capacity.

COMPETITION

You should include a word about your local competition. Not only should you specify the number of personal trainers, but you should also determine if they are in direct competition. If you are providing primarily weight-reduction services for the obese, you should not list as direct competition those personal trainers working exclusively with athletes. While the two services may involve similar exercises, they target two different types of people.

Any lenders you approach will be curious as to how large the potential market is in your area and how many trainers are attempting to tap into that market. You will have to demonstrate that there is an ample supply of potential clients for all personal trainers. If you find a heavily contested small pool of clients, you should consider either changing your market or relocating to a more amenable area with more uncontested potential clients who will seek your services.

THE TOP SEVEN SUGGESTIONS FOR NEW PERSONAL TRAINERS

1. Be open to suggestions.

2. Be willing to create a viable business. Some new trainers have many unique ideas about the way the business should be run. You need to be willing to create a personal training business that follows some conventional rules so that you can be successful. As you grow, you can become more creative and trendsetting.

3. Do not try to reinvent the system. The personal trainer business is a viable business already. Make sure your marketing plan works and that you are creating a business that will have potential to succeed and grow. Do not delude yourself and ignore your market analysis.

4. Be open and give your clients the opportunity to give you feedback. A simple survey at the end of a session is helpful. Listen to your clients' wants and needs rather than imposing what you believe they want and need. If your clients feel that they are being heard, it will raise their opinion of your service, which will translate to a greater number of future sales.

5. Use your business plan. If you spend time creating and writing it, do not just put it in a drawer when you are done. Believe in it and use it. Successful personal trainers follow and alter their plan as they go. It helps keep you on track and focused on finances and how you planned to do business.

6. Stick with your resolve. Even if you may end up being wrong, see it through. If you need to make changes along the way, that is fine, but if you do not try, you can never learn.

7. Do not be stubborn. Ask for help when needed. You may be a solo act when it comes to actual personal training, but you may need others to help you along the way. Your business plan is the best way to communicate with others where you need help. It is the blueprint of your operations. With this operations manual, other professionals can quickly assess and help you when you need help and make suggestions about how to make things run smoothly and efficiently.

TEST YOUR IDEA WITH A BUSINESS PLAN

You should begin putting your ideas and concepts on paper. You can start by tackling each of the above categories and penciling in your ideas. These ideas can be broadened later as you better understand the concepts with which you are working. When dealing with financial planning, you need to make accurate estimates of the investments you must initially make (e.g., equipment and rental space) along with the expenses you will encounter (e.g., water, electricity, and expendables, such as towels and soap). Then estimate how many clients, with how many hours of services each, you will initially be providing. A conservative guess will give you the rough amount of income demanded to meet expenses.

What is left over after all expenses is your gross profit. You must then allow for your tax, Social Security payments, any retirement funding, and other personal expenses. After everything is paid, your net profit is the remainder. Do not worry too much if there is no profit, as it often takes a new business more than two years to start earning one.

Ask yourself whether you have enough income from other resources to support yourself and the business enterprise until your company becomes profitable. If not, you have just discovered the number-one reason why relatively few people attempt to start a business, and the reason why many businesses fail within two years of their establishment.

Do not be among the new business failures. Planning for success is your strongest tool for maturing your personal training business into a successful operation. Planning, knowledge, skills, and abilities, when properly nurtured, will carry you through adversity to eventual victory.

Having explored this far into the inspection of your ability to start a successful business in personal training, you are ready to continue into Chapter 2 and discover how to acquire the knowledge necessary to practice the profession.

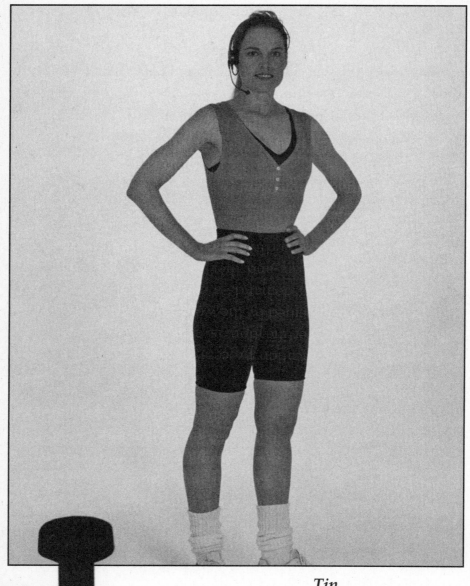

Tip

Try to do a cardio workout and weight lifting training on separate days. If this is not possible, then it is best to do your cardio workout after you have lifted weights.

Learning the Craft

2

Every person seeking to practice a skilled profession must acquire at least a basic knowledge of that profession prior to entering the field. To be certified as a personal trainer, you must exhibit a basic amount of knowledge and understanding. Accrediting organizations have established testing guidelines that fulfill this prerequisite.

The testing and certification process assures the consumer that whoever holds the certification is capable of performing the service at the level specified by the wording of the certificate. The certifying organization demands a certain level of competence in return for certification, and they are indirectly guaranteeing the consumer that those certified have the ability to perform that particular service at that level.

Accrediting organizations are respected third parties, and reassuring entities in which to place trust. This certification process is being used increasingly on a global scale and works well. Yet the ability to pass this basic level of testing will only allow you to enter the personal training profession at the most basic level. If you have any desire to improve your abilities or increase the scope of your practice, increasing your knowledge and experience base is the path you must follow.

In the personal trainer field, there are several means of acquiring the knowledge base necessary to start providing services. If you are interested in entering the business at its most basic level, the requirements will include being of a majority age (18 in most areas), having a high school diploma, having a basic knowledge of human anatomy, and possessing a rudimentary knowledge of resistance and cardiopulmonary training, along with a familiarity with resistance training equipment. Most employers will require CPR and perhaps First Aid certification, for which training is obtained separately from the personal trainer certification process.

This primitive level of certification can be acquired with no more than a few hours of individual training provided (at your cost) from the certifying agency. This will allow you to apply for jobs and provide services. However, this book was written in anticipation of your establishing your own business. In order to do this, a level of competence much higher than that of a simple employee will be required. There are several levels of knowledge acquisition involved. Four types of learning opportunities are presented here: apprenticeship, online training programs, formalized college or university education with internships, and various types of other training and traditional schools.

Each educational opportunity will be briefly described in terms of duration, learning environment, and course content.

APPRENTICESHIP

Apprenticeship is a traditional method of training a new generation of skilled practitioners. The apprentice works for an experienced professional, called a mentor, until the apprentice has sufficient skills to be declared a professional. An apprenticeship is an attractive training option. A modern apprenticeship combines education, on-the-job training, and practical experience — all while paying an entry-level wage.

Various sizes of organizations offer apprenticeships. You can choose from among individuals, well versed and willing to share their knowledge, to large, multicampus companies employing hundreds of trainers.

Many attractive training locations offer apprentice positions to promising young personal trainers. It is effective for employers in that it allows them to train personnel to their own specifications, thereby providing a steady pool of trained replacement employees. For the novice trainer, it is an opportunity to learn the trade "from the inside" of a well-established, successful organization.

You will be more likely to be offered a full-time position after a successful apprenticeship than someone approaching the company off the street. Being trained by the company instantly differentiates you from all competition for the position. You know how to conduct your training practice in the exact manner expected by your employer. If you can locate a program very similar to the business model you wish to establish, apprenticing to that program would bring you an unparalleled opportunity to absorb valuable knowledge in a targeted manner.

Apprenticeship programs can be closely allied with colleges, universities, and other training programs. These programs will offer employment, on-the-job training, and experience while you remain in classes for the formal educational portion of the curriculum. The attraction of such a program is that you will not only receive certification and experience, but a degree as well. This will enhance your future employment possibilities and your chances of success when you start your own business in personal training.

Duration

An apprenticeship can be as short as a few months and extend as long as two to four years. Some apprentice programs are designed to take the new trainer from an entry level, through several additional levels, to the position of master trainer. Traditionally, an apprentice would serve under a master of the skill until the master decided that the student had mastered all phases and could serve as a journeyman in the craft. Modern apprenticeship programs will generally have clearly delineated goals and timelines stated prior to any commitments. If you are contemplating working as an apprentice, find out exactly what will be expected of you and get that on paper prior to any firm commitment. You should get an approximate time line for completion of the program.

Learning Environment

In most cases, an apprenticeship will be served in the same locale as personal trainer services are performed. Regardless of the environment in which your employer provides services, you will be expected to participate. An attractive aspect of an apprenticeship is that the entire training period can be listed as practical experience on your resume.

Your apprenticeship program is a form of employment in which you receive a cash remuneration, experience, and knowledge for your labor. The combination of these is your actual total "income." The knowledge you gain is stored away in your mind in much the same way you would set aside a portion of earnings in a savings account. This knowledge income is of more value than the cash income. The knowledge will serve you well for your lifetime.

Course Content

When selecting an apprenticeship program, you should seek out a program that most closely resembles the practice you wish to pursue when finished. Not that you want to have an apprentice, but that the services will be delivered in an environment similar to those in which you want to work. An effective apprenticeship should be an extension of your life's work — a foundation, so to speak, on which to build your personal practice.

If you want to employ several trainers eventually, you should look for someone who will include training in basic business practices, marketing, and some business accounting. All phases of the business you anticipate to encounter in your own company should be covered in the apprenticeship. You should be taught the basics of managing your future employees and how to effectively deal with customers.

An apprenticeship should include those basic elements required for your certification. This should be the foundation, and additional knowledge and experience will build upon that. Prior to enrollment, ask whether certification is an incremental element in the flow of coursework or the product. Accreditation as a personal trainer should be a starting point of an apprenticeship, not an end goal. There is much to learn after your credentialing.

An apprenticeship can also be combined with other types of training or schooling. If you find your training lacking in a particular area, you may wish to take some specialized courses to fill in the gaps. This would allow you to apprentice yourself to an otherwise good program that lacks some rudiments of the education you desire. Throughout your lifetime, you will probably use all forms of training at one time or another, as no one form will provide the perfect solution.

ONLINE TRAINING PROGRAMS

The fastest-growing training format is online. Logging onto the Internet with a browser and receiving courses electronically is a growing industry. It is a convenient way to learn the personal training craft. With new technologies such as conferencing and instant messaging (IM), even interpersonal interactions rival those of traditional classroom settings.

The online classroom can range from an individual reading through materials appearing on their monitor, to a virtual, real-time classroom with many students interacting with an instructor in a multidimensional experience. Traditional higher-education institutions such as universities have joined the online education revolution. They offer programs ranging from certification to bachelor's degree, with virtually all classroom interaction conducted through the Internet. With this endorsement of confidence, other organizations have quickly followed suit and now offer their own programs.

Programs available online vary greatly. At the lowest end, simple certification instruction is offered by organizations of sometimes little reputation or experience in the field. Some offer little more than instruction found elsewhere at little or no cost. Most major certification programs and associations now offer online coursework in conjunction with their certifications. At the upper end is university training with a four-year degree program.

Programs offered online for $50 and less should be viewed with suspicion, unless they are continuing education classes offered by accredited institutions or associations. A site offering "guaranteed" success when taking a certification exam may be selling you an antiquated book with little assistance to you and no recourse to recover your money. Be sure to deal with only established institutions and associations, well-known in the personal trainer industry.

Duration

Online training programs will vary from just a few days in duration to university programs that involve four or more years of study. In general, the longer the program lasts, the more in-depth and broader of scope will be the information taught. That which holds in the "real" world will be true in the online medium. There are no "miracles" of an instant education simply because a program originates online.

You should expect to spend roughly the same amount of time accomplishing the same goals online as you would physically attending classroom instruction; however, you will be able to do this from the comfort of your own home. Considering the distances to some training facilities, you may find a savings in total costs if you had to commute or find an apartment to reside in while training. In attending online universities, there is a considerable cost savings in commuting and living expenses.

Learning Environment

The physical environment for an online course is your own home, or whatever location you choose. In the case of online studies, the environment may also be expanded to include the electronic class format.

The educator may choose to have simple Web pages with educational content. In this case, you would simply read the page and interact with any other content, including tests and workbooks. Automated feedback systems include online forms, testing systems, and a combination of multidimensional systems. Audio and video content can also be programmed into the coursework.

IM can be used for occasional contact between instructor and student or as a format for an entire class. IM is similar to working over a telephone line. IM can be a cold environment if neither party is able to enliven the atmosphere. Online conferencing has the potential to add video and audio, which enhances the interaction.

Online conferencing requires a broadband connection for both parties. Many areas, especially rural ones, have yet to access this high-speed Internet capability. If you have access to a broadband connection, this can be an attractive alternative to physically attending classes. Those who rely heavily upon nonverbal interaction with others, that is, observation of body and facial movement, often find this type of interaction unsatisfactory.

Prior to committing yourself to a lengthy online training program, you should test yourself for compatibility to that learning environment. Even the most interesting subjects require an ability to focus for some length of time on reading and interacting with the computer. If you can become so absorbed in the course that you forget you are working with a machine, you will probably do well working online.

Course Content

Online courses contain all the elements available through traditional education and training programs, with the exception of physical interaction. In learning a trade such as personal trainer, this lack of physical interaction can be a severe limitation. As physical contact and observation is at the heart of the profession, you might consider combining online work with an internship with a local employer. This would provide you with both practical experience and instruction.

Some programs will offer you local practical experience, but you should be prepared to find your own internship situation. Other practical information that should be incorporated into an online educational program includes customer service, ongoing support, and testing and exam options. You should also learn as much as possible about the instructors you will be using — their background, experience, education, and training/teaching styles.

If you are enrolling in one of the many certification associations, ask how many personal trainers they have certified and how well those trainers fare in the marketplace. A reputable firm will be proud to supply you with information and even contacts among their graduates. If they attempt to dodge difficult questions, you may need to seek other organizations for your purposes.

For some of the best online exercise science and graduate fitness programs available, search Distance.GradSchools.com at **programs.gradschools.com/distance/kinesiology.html**.

Whatever source you choose for your educational and training needs, find out whether they provide ongoing training to increase your knowledge base. You will need continuing education classes to keep up to date with the latest personal trainer information, as this industry is in continual growth.

Expect at least as much from an online training institution as you would from standard brick and mortar facilities. The purpose in seeking an education is to improve yourself, not to circumvent the system. Any organization that promises to certify you with minimal personal effort on your part should be avoided.

COLLEGE/UNIVERSITY EDUCATION

The attraction of formal education is manifold. You will receive the most thorough and well-rounded education available. You will not only be trained in the specialty of personal training, but in ancillary subjects, such as business administration, accounting procedures, and other fields vital to supporting your new business ventures.

One of the most lasting benefits of a two- to four-year degree program is the impression it makes upon those who will prove pivotal to your fledgling business pursuits, such as lending institutions and new clientele. A person who has completed a degree program at an accredited university or college has shown that they are capable of successfully tackling a large job with long-range goals. This is important to individuals and organizations attempting to judge the potential for success or failure of your proposed business venture. Even in your attempts to secure an internship appointment, your dedication to succeed in school will positively influence prospective employers.

With the ultimate goal of successfully managing your own future business, your training and education will largely influence your success. The more rounded your education, the better will be your chances of succeeding. Working with clients as a trainer will become an increasingly smaller portion of your workday as your business grows to include additional trainers. You will find yourself increasingly forced into the position of business manager as your growing business becomes more successful.

Few people in our modern society remain in static positions as our grandparents once did. Formerly an individual might have found employment as a youngster in a particular job category and remain in that position, often with the same employer, for a lifetime. In your own career, you will likely hold positions in at least three to four differing job categories, in a smoothly flowing transition of tasks.

You might enter the personal trainer field as an entry-level trainer in an internship position, become a full-time employee learning the ropes or the profession and the business, then become a supervisor, combining your practice with overseeing the efforts of other trainers and teaching newcomers. Eventually, you will feel comfortable establishing your own business, at which point you are mainly a personal trainer again with some management responsibilities. As time passes and you add employees and clientele, you may find that your day is filled with business-related concerns. You have become a business executive so gradually, you have little recollection of the transition between tasks.

The important part is recognizing that your end goals require more than training as an expert in exercise disciplines. To succeed in the goal of establishing a business, especially a large business, you must have expertise in a broad variety of subjects. To accomplish this end, you must seek out educational opportunities that offer training in these varied tasks. The best source of this type of educational opportunity is a university education.

Duration

Colleges and universities offer two- and four-year degree programs in addition to post-graduate level master's and doctoral degrees. A two-year associate's degree will likely be in a specialized program with the aim of preparing a personal trainer to fill an entry-level position. While it does not offer a starting position higher than less intensive programs, it will represent a better-rounded education.

Four-year baccalaureate degrees will not only include a well-rounded education in a variety of subjects, but also the opportunity to become highly specialized in particular therapeutic subjects. Some exacting licensed trades, such as rehabilitation therapy, require a four-year degree for certification and entry into the field.

At the master's level, you will acquire even more specialized abilities to serve populations with handicaps and disabilities. These people have issues that demand extremely specialized knowledge. If you acquire a doctoral degree (PhD), you will be qualified to work with people with virtually any set of needs. In addition, you will be well qualified for teaching positions. A PhD is the goal of an individual with high ambitions.

Learning Environment

Most graduates of colleges and universities agree that an attractive part of the degree programs is the surrounding environment of the university. From the dormitories or apartments to extra-curricular activities, such as football and basketball, these people enjoy immersing themselves in the learning, the people, and the traditions of college life.

Higher education will normally fit into the semester format. You enroll in a set of courses that will last about three to four months, at the end of which you repeat the process until completion. Personal training degrees will have a set of "core" classes, within degree curriculum guidelines, required by most underclassmen. In the junior and senior years, you will select elective classes to specialize your abilities. It is likely you will be required to fulfill some type of internship. This will be the practical portion of your experience.

Along with coursework leading to your exercise training expertise, you have the opportunity to study other courses that will build your business knowledge. These elective courses can even lead to a "minor" in Business Administration. Business is a complex world that you must learn to navigate to become successful. The university staff can prepare you to run your business.

Course Content

All colleges and universities have common and unique classes and degree programs. While most offer similar classes at a lower level, they differ greatly in the more specialized types of coursework.

This gives the entering student an opportunity to match their interests to the university that offers the best opportunity to pursue those specialized interests.

Be prepared for the most common complaint heard from freshmen and sophomores — that they are required to take courses useless to them. In actuality, these lower-level "core" curriculum courses lay a valuable groundwork of knowledge that allows the individual to build upon it in any direction their life may take. As previously mentioned, most people will smoothly transition into more than one profession. Without prior knowledge of the exact direction a student's future career will take, universities prepare students to adapt themselves in whatever position they eventually fall into.

Indeed, a major responsibility laid upon the university by society is to prepare students not only for their professional careers, but for life in general. Learning to be effective citizens, good neighbors, and to raise good families is at least as important as making a good living.

If you are interested in universities with exercise science programs, please refer to All Allied Health Schools at **www.allalliedhealth-schools.com/featured/exercise-science/?src=goo_ahs_hlth_ftns_111006_50756b.**

OTHER TRAINING/EDUCATIONAL OPPORTUNITIES

In this category, we find the "trial and error" approach to learning to become a personal trainer. If you have no law or local code requiring certification at your location, you can simply declare that you are a personal trainer and start providing services. As you gain clients and experience, you will learn which practices work for your clients and which do not. If you are lucky, you might be able to build a client base in this manner.

You and your clients will be better served, however, if you find some source of knowledge prior to presenting yourself to the public as an expert in fitness. There is also the prospect of injuring your clients. A basic knowledge of anatomy and what stresses the human body can take in various fitness conditions will be helpful. If you injure a client through a lack of knowledge, you will be liable for that injury and the negative impact it causes in your client's life. Should a lawsuit develop, this liability can quickly overwhelm your financial situation, not to mention the burden it lays upon your conscience.

The responsibility of providing effective, intelligent services is the primary reason that gyms, fitness clubs, and other employers of personal trainers demand certification of trainers as proof of at least a basic level of competence. Their insurance providers might also demand proof of competence.

You must also be careful in selecting the type of certification you seek. Be sure that you match the type of certification offered by the certifying agency with the needs of a prospective employer or the needs or your own company's clients. There are hundreds of specific certifications you can obtain. If you gain certification as a corporate wellness/fitness trainer while attempting to gain employment as a sports trainer of some type, your time consuming labors to become certified will gain you little.

When planning your educational and training efforts, you should define your short- (personal trainer) and long-term (business management) goals. Plan your education around these goals to best prepare yourself for the future. Try to gain at least a basic instruction in all topics you can foresee a need to practice in your future. It will serve you better to be over-prepared than to be lacking in knowledge.

3 Planning Your Approach

At this point, you are certain that personal training is the career for you. There is no doubt that this is the field in which you wish to spend your working life. Now, exactly how do you propose to enter this chosen field?

TYPES OF BUSINESS RELATIONSHIPS

There are three basic choices for you here: employment as a personal trainer, collaborating with other trainers, or starting your own business. This book is all about starting you own business, but it would be irresponsible not to consider all avenues to reaching this goal. Each individual must make a personal assessment of their life to decide just what course of action is most appropriate at this starting point of his or her career.

Along with your own intellectual and physical readiness, you must also consider your financial situation and family obligations. It would be negligent to ignore the financial and other needs of a growing family should you start a business without the necessary resources to support you until your business becomes profitable.

In addition, a new start-up business is extremely time-intensive. You will need to spend many hours in not only personal training, but also marketing your new enterprise to gain enough clients to become self-sustaining.

BENEFITS AS AN EMPLOYEE

There are many incentives to hiring yourself out to establish your reputation prior to starting your own business. Chief among these benefits is a regular paycheck. Another benefit for a new trainer is the fact the company will provide all equipment and work space without any investment on your part. Health insurance is also important for a young family. Independent personal trainers will have to spend heavily to secure health coverage, especially if they obtain insurance covering childbirth.

As an employee, you will likely receive annual vacation and sick leave. A retirement plan is another plus. In addition, you will have to spend very little time on administrative overhead — the largest amount of time, energy, and money consumed in the management of a small business. All these benefits make being an employee attractive, but there are drawbacks.

As an employee, you will have little say in the running of the business. Your income will be limited to your hours worked and to sporadic pay increases. You will probably have little choice as to what hours you work. Perhaps most frustrating is that your employer will be taking a significant portion of the income you generate.

However, being an employee for even a short amount of time can act as an effective launch pad for your business career. It will allow you time to get your skill sets into good shape, prepare yourself financially, and learn the finer points of the personal training business. In addition, you will begin gaining a reputation and a client base. Be careful, though, when signing on as an employee at a gym. They may require that you sign a no-competition agreement. This means that when you leave, you cannot take any of your clients with you.

Carefully observing a successful training business from the inside out is a very valuable means of learning the trade. Your employer will likely have discovered the best ways of managing the business and established the most effective business practices. Your job is not only to be a good employee, but also to dedicate yourself to learning all you can while exposed to these successful methods.

Education is the practice of accumulating knowledge of those who have gone before so that you may build upon that knowledge base. What better way to establish a profitable business than by learning from someone who has already shown they can operate one? If you carefully choose a company for which to work that has exhibited its ability to carry on a thriving personal trainer business, you can duplicate these methods and practices when you reach the point of starting your own company.

View employment not as an end in itself, but as a logical step in the evolution from worker to employer and business owner. Few successful business owners went directly from student to businessperson. The smart ones sought out the best mentors and worked under them until they felt fully prepared to enter the business world.

PARTNERSHIPS

At some point, you will feel qualified to strike out on your own. This can be a scary moment. When you start working exclusively for yourself, you move into uncertain territory. There is a way to remove some of the loneliness of this moment. You can partner with one or more of your friends or coworkers. Besides the companionship, there is strength in sharing. You will have someone to talk to and confide in as well as others who can lend strength in bad times. Pooling of knowledge and resources yields a much higher chance of success.

Partnerships have traditionally been hard to sustain. There are numerous stories of failed partner operations and friends becoming enemies after working together. These issues do arise, but a partnership built upon good business practices between two mature adults stands a good chance of success. Do not fear collaborating with someone because of rumors, but do establish the relationship based on good business practices, not strictly on personal relationships.

Partners can share equipment costs, rents, administrative overhead, and even cover for each other in an emergency. Probably the most important consideration is the mutual sharing of the experience. You are not alone; you do have company. A partner can back you up with knowledge and other valuable resources. You will have someone with whom to toss around ideas and who will give you advice. Finally, partners can help broaden the services the partnership can offer. You can help each other to cover all the bases.

A partnership can be an inexpensive means to starting a business. This is especially true if you find someone willing to collaborate with you because his or her customer base has outgrown that person's ability to handle it alone. This overflow of clients can be just the thing to get you going with a minimum amount of time lost to building a business. You can simply walk into an established clientele. Groups of partners are often built around this progressive growth of a business.

ENTRY POINTS

This chapter will look at some possible entry points for your new personal training career. There are several alternatives well worth your consideration as possible avenues to getting that all-important income flowing into your business. After all, without sufficient income to sustain yourself and possibly your family, you cannot long remain in business.

Places you can operate your personal training business include home, a private personal training studio, clients' home gyms, or corporate fitness centers. Many personal trainers earn an average of $30 to $100 per hour. This book will teach you all you need to know about starting your own business in minimal time.

FINDING A NICHE

Specialization is a highly recommended path to establishing yourself in the personal training field. Few trainers present themselves as experts in all possible areas of personal training; those who do have generally overestimated their abilities. By this point, you have probably isolated one or more areas of personal training that interest you above all others. Perhaps the service areas you have been working in are the ones you feel most comfortable offering to the public.

After a little thought, pick that one area in which you have the highest interest and in which you feel best qualified. We are not talking about spending your entire life in this particular niche; we are looking for an entry point. That entry point should represent the best possible choice for your success at this time in your life.

Let us assume you love sports and work well with people active in the various types of activities with which you are associated. You not only know what specific exercises and equipment are vital, but you already have established contacts locally. You know the players and possibly the various coaches. This makes it an ideal entry point for you.

Another example might be that your aging parents have brought you into contact with a seniors' training program. You have helped not only your parents, but also several of their friends to set up exercise programs to maximize their health. You have found this not only interesting, but you get a good feeling helping these people get the most out of their golden years.

A third example is working with youth. You may have volunteered to work with a little league team. It does not take long before the enthusiasm of these children inspires you. You may find the excitement of a little league game irresistible. There are numerous niche training activities available in the youth market for personal trainers.

Look around your town. Observe the populations that other personal training professionals are serving and spot the opportunities that have been overlooked. These niche opportunities are always there; it just takes a little creative imagination to see them. Once you have observed an opportunity, talk to some potential consumers about your services. Find out if there is a market there for what you have to offer. Determine if there are enough potential clients to make it worth your while, or if you could expand the niche to include other possible opportunities.

Let us say you have targeted a community of seniors who desire to improve their general health and longevity. Once you have signed up a few of them, you find the market is not as broad and deep as expected. Now you reach out to the middle-aged children of your seniors with an offer of better cardiovascular health. Your first clients are now acting as a sales force for your modified services.

The point here is that whatever grabs you most — that which creates a passion within you — is your best possible choice for getting started in the personal trainer business. What passion can you pass on to your clients if you cannot become excited yourself? You will work harder, create excitement in others, and find much greater happiness if you are doing what you love.

You do not have to find the passion of your life at this particular moment, but the niche you choose should represent some particular activity in which you have a superior knowledge and at least some experience. No one is going to spend their hard-earned money for someone to repeat to them information they already know. You will be hired because you have valuable information.

Once you have determined what you want your niche to be, check local demographics. The obvious places to find clients are where people work out, but there are other places to consider, like health food markets, vitamin shops, and doctor's offices. You will have to look for clients; do not expect them to know you are in business just because you made business cards and have set up a Web site.

Your choice of client will determine the type of business you establish and where you do your marketing. The term "demographics" refers to the characteristics of the people in your target audience. Demographics reveal who is more likely to use your services or products. Some of the characteristics you may want to consider are the age of people you are targeting, their income level, where they live, the type of personal training services they might want, and their education level. When you determine your clients' demographics, you will be able to determine where you need to seek them out.

An important demographic to consider is age. This demographic is important because, if you are spending your time and effort on women in their early twenties, you may be wasting valuable time and resources if you live near a retirement community. Once you have determined whether your preferred age group is near you, you can decide on a marketing strategy. If this age group is not present, you many need to rethink your business options. This does not mean that all is lost if there is not a large population of people in their late twenties. It just means that you need to look at gyms and other places to find women in that age group.

You could decide that older people will be the demographic that you will target. Many older men and women are looking at fitness as the key to their longevity and quality of life. They may need your guidance and expertise to help them. For some, it could be the first time they have formally exercised in their life.

Another demographic to consider is people with a certain income. They have three things that can work to your advantage:

1. They have the money to spend on fitness, and especially on a personal trainer.

2. They do not have the time to try to organize their workout routine because of their jobs.

3. They know the value of outsourcing to professionals.

People in a higher tax bracket have more flexibility when it comes to spending money. This gives them the freedom and resources to hire a professional to help them get fit.

Most people with higher incomes do not have the time to figure out what machines to use or what they should be eating to trim their waistline. They have careers and do not want to give up precious time reading health books and figuring out what diets they should be on. They would rather have someone else do it for them. This can translate into more money in your pocket.

Successful businesspeople become successful because they know how to delegate jobs. They know that when something needs to be done and everyone is busy, they may need to outsource certain projects. That is why it is natural for them to a hire a personal trainer to help them get into shape.

If you intend to make a living as a personal trainer, you have to consider whether the demographic you have chosen can afford you. You can conduct some research on your own to see whether personal training is viable in your area. You can do a couple of different kinds of research: primary and secondary.

PRIMARY RESEARCH

The information collected in primary research is original and collected for a specific purpose. The problem with primary research is that it can be expensive and time consuming. The benefit over secondary research is that it is more focused. There are a few ways you can conduct your own primary research on personal training:

- Telephone interviews

- Face-to-face interviews

- Internet surveys

- Mystery shopping

Telephone Interviews

These types of interviews are structured, but they can lack depth. The advantages of telephone interviews are that they can target a geographic area or be spread over large geographical areas, they are relatively inexpensive, and you can collect a random sampling of people. The disadvantages of telephone interviews are that respondents often hang up, the interviews are short, no visual aids can be used, and you cannot glean any information by behavior or body language.

Face-to-Face Interviews

Face-to face interviews are more intimate than other interviews. Advantages of face-to-face interviews are that they can be more in-depth, you can use pictures, and other aides to assist you, and you can gather more information through behavior and body language. The disadvantages of face-to-face interviews are that they can be more costly, they can take time to arrange and conduct, and sometimes, the data is not reliable because the person being interviewed wants to please the interviewer.

The Internet

The Internet is used in a number of ways to conduct surveys. These usually appear as questionnaires on Web sites, and they often offer incentives for people to complete the surveys. Some of the advantages of Internet surveys are that they are relatively inexpensive, they can use visual aides, and people are willing to fill them out because they like the site where they located the survey. There are disadvantages of using the Internet to conduct surveys, such as not knowing how to use the software to create them, being unable to place them on fitness sites that would be the best place to use such a survey, and that some people do not like them and view them as an invasion of privacy.

Mail Survey

This may be the most common, easiest way for a personal trainer to conduct a market survey. You can do this by purchasing a mailing list that is targeted to the market in which you wish to do research. You can buy these lists from trade associations, newspapers, or Internet list brokers. You can request lists in a specific geographical area where you wish to start your personal trainer business. You may want to consider the following criteria when you have a company build a list for you:

1. Age

2. Gender

3. Profession

4. Health risk

5. Weight

There are a number of options to choose from. The more superior the list you buy, the better survey results you will receive. Here are a couple of places to look at for obtaining mailing lists.

- Ⴕ **www.srds.com.** This company specializes in providing information about publications that sell their mailing lists in the Standard Rate and Data service.

- Ⴕ **www.marketingsource.com.** This company creates and sells direct mailing lists according to your specifications.

- Ⴕ **www.caldwell-list.com.** This company produces custom mailing lists.

- Ⴕ **www.goleads.com**. This is another company that can use certain criteria to create the right mailing list for you.

Once you have the mailing list, you should create a questionnaire that addresses your marketing needs. After completing your questionnaire, print it out on your company letterhead and make copies. If you have an e-mail list, you can send the questionnaire via e-mail.

Be aware that when you buy certain mailing lists, they may be for one use only. They will be seeded with addresses that the company can monitor. If you send out more than one mailing using the list, you could be charged for using it again.

Offering cash is one incentive to get someone to take the survey and send it back to you through the mail. If you slip a dollar bill into the envelope, a person is more likely to spend the time to fill out the survey. If you have thousands of addresses, this could become too costly. This research is very important because you will use the data you gather to tailor your personal trainer business and the services it offers. In the end, it can earn you more money in less time if you target just the right market.

Mystery Shopping

This is something you can do on your own. Call around to other personal trainers and set up appointments. Find out what their services are and how they do business. If they charge a fee for a consultation, you need to figure that into your research budget. You can gather important information from your competition.

Marketing Firms

If you do not feel comfortable conducting the research yourself and you have a good-sized budget, consider hiring a marketing firm to do your research. They can charge between $2,000 and $8,000, depending on what type of research you want them to conduct. They do have the expertise to conduct this kind of research on your behalf, and they may have access to tools and resources that you do not. They can conduct the research, collect the data, analyze it, and put all of the results in a report for you.

SECONDARY RESEARCH

This type of research is affordable and can be done more quickly than primary research. You are essentially using outside agencies and reports to conduct your research. The drawback is that the research could have been done for other purposes than what you intend to use it for. It can be unfocused and difficult to use for what you need. Here is a list of possible sources of secondary research:

- Trade associations

- National and local press industry magazines

- National/international governments

- Informal contacts

- Trade directories

- Published company accounts

- Business libraries

- Professional institutes and organizations

- Previously gathered marketing research

- Census data

- Public records

A few Web sites provide the necessary information:

- **www.census.gov.** The U. S. Census Bureau's official site.

- **www.sba.gov.** The U. S. Small Business Administration's site.

- **jmc.ou.edu/FredBeard/Secondary.html.** This site contains many links for sources of secondary research information.

After gathering your data, you must decide how to use it. It should give you a clear idea of who your target market is. In addition, it should give you a clear idea where to best use your resources in advertising and marketing. You will know who your clients are, what they are looking for, and where to find them.

A poor understanding of the personal trainer market — the industry and target clientele — can be the weakest part of a personal trainer's business plans. There is a direct correlation between the success of your business and your awareness of changing trends, technology, scientific advances, competitors, and what your clients are looking for. It is up to you to analyze trends, needs, and statistics. This will keep your business in competition with changing markets, and you will be able to adjust your business plan quickly so that you do not lag behind.

You now should have identified a niche in which you have expertise and little competition. If there is an intense competition to providing that service, you should consider altering your plans. Fortunately, there are ways to change the service enough to avert a clash with other providers. If you have chosen to work with inner-city youth, you may wish to adjust your service marketing to middle-class youth with weight problems. This slight change may make a big difference in finding clients.

In order to understand the personal trainer industry and your competition, you must learn as much as you can about the following:

- Who your competition is

- New fitness and health trends

- Entry barriers

- Exit barriers

- Industry analysis, trends, and statistics

COMPETITION

Make a list of all your major competitors. These can be grouped geographically or by services offered. After you have made your list, use the Personal Trainer Competition Analysis worksheet to analyze your competition.

PERSONAL TRAINER COMPETITION ANALYSIS WORKSHEET

1. The number of personal trainers in your area is:

   Many   Some   Few   Unknown

2. The competition is dominated by several large personal trainer gyms/companies.

   Yes   No   Unknown

3. The combined market share of the three largest personal trainer businesses is:

   <40 percent   40–80 percent   >80 percent   Unknown

4. New technology and equipment change every:

   Year   Five Years   Ten Years   Unknown

5. The barriers that stop new competitors from entering the personal trainer business are:

   High   Medium   Low   Unknown

6. Overall market demand in the personal trainer industry is:

   Growing   Stable   Declining   Unknown

7. There is a large, untapped market in the personal trainer industry that you can find a niche in.

   Yes   Maybe   No   Unknown

8. The personal trainer industry offers different options as far as the type of services that a personal trainer can offer.

   Extensive   Average   Limited   Unknown

PERSONAL TRAINER COMPETITION ANALYSIS WORKSHEET

9. Clients buy personal trainer services based almost entirely on price.

   Yes   No   Unknown

10. Clients can use other types of services without using personal trainer services to get fit.

   Easily   With Difficulty   No   Unknown

11. Personal trainers in your area have much influence when it comes to setting terms and prices on consulting.

   Yes   No   Unknown

12. Clients have much bargaining power when contracting for personal trainer services.

   Yes   No   Unknown

13. Gym owners have much power and play a major role in the workings of the personal trainer industry.

   Yes   No   Unknown

14. The overall prices in the personal trainer industry have been:

   Rising   Stable   Declining   Unknown

15. The profit margins in personal training are:

   Strong   Average   Weak   Unknown

The answers on this worksheet should give you a better understanding of the personal trainer industry in your area and your competition. If you marked any of the answers "unknown," you need to do further research.

FITNESS TRENDS AND TECHNOLOGY

The ever-changing trends, technology, and science associated with health and fitness are a major driver of the personal trainer industry. In this section, we will discuss how much the changing face of fitness will drive your business, how fast it is changing, who controls and sets the standards for health and fitness, and how easily you can get information and products associated with the new trends in fitness training.

ENTRY BARRIERS

The barriers that prevent new competitors from setting up their own personal training business are referred to as entry barriers. Some examples of these barriers may be the lack of capital, a small client base, geographical limitations, and ways to reach clients. There is the economy of scale to consider. This principle states that the bigger your company is, the more money you will make because larger companies can do business cheaper than small business and therefore can offer lower prices. These lower prices translate into more clients. An example of this is that a local pizza company that makes a pizza for $10 cannot compete with larger national chains that can make a similar pizza for $5. This can discourage sole proprietors from entering the personal training industry. Established businesses with a strong client base and money for keeping up with new equipment and technology trends can be daunting competitors to some would-be personal trainers.

EXIT BARRIERS

If you decide you do not want to continue personal training, there may be obstacles that make it difficult for you to get out; these are referred to as exit barriers. If you have invested your life savings and borrowed extensively to get the business going, it may be difficult to call it quits. You may want to consider if there is any other market, such as nutrition and health products, that you could get into where you could easily shift your company's focus. Knowing all that you can about the personal trainer business can be to your advantage.

A successful businessperson must have a liberal amount of flexibility. Anticipation of changes in the field and the ability to alter course before being negatively impacted by those changes is the hallmark of good business practices. If there is one critical issue you will face as a businessperson, it is that an ever-changing environment will be your continual companion. Look upon change as an opportunity for future success. It is an effective means to differentiate you from other personal trainers. Your clientele will recognize your abilities and success will reward your efforts.

Speaking of your ability to adapt, where will you be providing your services? Chances are that your clients will not possess a complete home gym. Alternatives abound in this area. Public and private gyms and workout areas dot the landscape in most metropolitan areas, and even smaller cities and towns have at least one or two established exercise businesses. Membership fees may be an issue to either your client or yourself.

Be flexible. Work in your client's home or perhaps your own; set up an extra bedroom as a workspace. You can supply needed equipment or create an exercise regime that does not need equipment until you can find a way to supply it. In good weather, you can set up walking or running exercises in public parks or other areas with free access. At some point, you will have enough money to pay a good client's gym fees or even rent space to organize with the best equipment. Until that time, you will rely upon your wits and give your clients the impression that this exercise environment is the best idea for them at this time.

Another area requiring flexibility is time. You may have to work nights or early mornings. You left the nine-to-five life behind when you opted for self-employment. Working with clients at their convenience is not an option, it is a requirement — especially while getting started.

DEVELOPING A MARKETING PLAN

When you begin to think about marketing your personal trainer business, start with a wide view. Think about why you decided to form the business in the first place. What does your business have to offer a client that is unique and different from other trainers? Review your business statement and look specifically at your mission and values statements. Make sure that the description you form about your company is as clear and concise as possible. Your description should answer the following questions:

1. What makes you think that your personal training business will make money?

2. What is your formula for success?

3. What feedback have you gotten from current or past clients about the success of your business?

4. Have you made any contact with your competitors? What do they say about your business?

5. Is your personal training based upon the amount of money you are making per client or the number of clients you are working with?

6. What is the launch date of your business?

7. Is the personal trainer business the type of business that has busy or slow seasons?

8. What are business hours? Will you be scheduel be a set or flexible one?

9. Do you plan to have a home based or office based business?

10. Are you working with gyms? How will you contract professionals to work with you?

When you have a good description of your business structure, you will need to create a good description of the personal trainer services that you will be offering. These descriptions should be lively and attract attention. A person seeking a trainer should be able to get a clear mental image of your services by reading these descriptions. This will be important when these descriptions are included in marketing and advertising materials. If you plan to have people invest in your business, it is easier for them to make a decision when they have a clear image of the services you will be offering. When creating your descriptions, make sure the language is easy to read and free of jargon so the average person reading it will understand and grasp it quickly. Your descriptions should answer the following questions:

1. What services do you offer? These should be broken down individually with a complete description of each. If you have fitness plans, are you going to offer to break them down individually as well?

2. What does your service offer a client (i.e., a better body, better health, better self-image)?

3. What need does your personal trainer business fill (i.e., no trainers in the area, a gym needs a full-time personal trainer)?

4. Who are your customers? (This goes back to your demographics.)

5. How will the customer benefit from using your consulting service?

6. What makes your personal trainer business different from your competitor's?

7. What are the advantages and disadvantages of your service (i.e., you are working from home, you live far away from the gym, or there are not many workout places to choose from)?

8. What are the strengths and weaknesses of the services you will offer (i.e., prices, your experience)?

9. What will be the unique selling point you will use with potential clients (i.e., a catchy slogan, press releases, awards you have won)?

The next item you will need to develop is a business history and your personal experience. As this information will be seen by potential clients, it should be produced to impress. When a potential client reads it, it should make them want to hire you immediately. This is where you need to shine. Bragging and boasting, as long as it is well founded and honest, is encouraged.

You need to create a narrative about your business. It is the story about when, how, and why your business was born. This should be like telling an epic story, full of drama and excitement.

Here are two examples:

> **"One day while I was watching an ESPN show about bodybuilding, I thought to myself, 'Wow, I could do that.' So I borrowed some money from my family and here I am."**

> **"I had a vision. In that vision, I saw a man competing in a bodybuilding competition. He was all over the news. He had a wonderful story about how he had been unhealthy and overweight most of his life, but after he began to work with Joe Smith as a personal trainer, he not only shed the pounds, but was able to sculpt the body he had always dreamed of. Now he had won his first bodybuilding competition."**

Of course, the second paints a picture that some potential clients can relate to. It creates an image of a business that was created so the average person could have the body he or she had always dreamed of. The following suggestions will give you something to think about as you create the written history of your business:

You should include what the current status is of your business. This should state whether you are actively engaged in business or you are just starting out. You will be updating your company history to make it current. Every six months to a year is a good time frame. This can be more often if there are exciting additions or changes in your business, such as a famous client or an award your business has received.

You should include what type of business you have, such as a partnership, an LLC, or a sole proprietorship. This gives the reader an idea with whom they are dealing. If you have made any changes to this over time, you should state why. If there have been any changes in management or structure, such as adding employees, this should be included in your company history description.

Your narrative should list any milestones or setbacks your company may have experienced, such as moving to a new location or losing a partner. This should be a description of how this has affected your business and how it has helped you grow or change your focus.

Once you have completed your company history, you should include your biography and that of any other significant person involved in the company. Here are some dos and do nots for creating this kind of biography:

- **Do** include your education, job history (make sure it is relevant to personal training and fitness), and any experience that makes you the perfect trainer for a potential client.

- **Do** include who you worked for, how many events you have created, and any famous or influential people you have worked for.

- **Do not** exaggerate, make up past clients, or in any way be dishonest.

- **Do not** include irrelevant information, such as you once saw Chuck Norris working out at the gym you once belonged to.

You want to shine and be noticed. Make every effort to impress.

INTEGRATING THE BUSINESS PLAN

All the issues that influence your ability to attract clients and hold them is an integral part of your overall marketing plan. The plan consists of: (1) your services and what sets you apart from the competition; (2) your service pricing strategy; (3) your plan to sell yourself and your services to potential clients, as well as the when, where, and how of delivering your services; (4) and finally, promotional work and advertising efforts you plan to make.

The services portion of the plan is the service niche you have identified and are seeking to fill. A pricing plan is simple in the initial stages of your business. You will likely key your own service charges to those of your competition. If you do not know what other personal trainers are charging for similar services, find out. You will have to do the math to assure yourself you are charging enough to cover expenses and put a profit into your pocket. No one can operate at a loss for long. Also, do not be afraid to charge a sufficient wage; you and your services have value. The most common reason trainers find themselves underpaid is that they simply did not ask for higher fees.

An easy way to decide upon a fee schedule is to take the average of all personal trainers you can find fee information about in your area. You may have already done this as a mystery shopper while doing your demographics. The average price is a good starting point. Should you find that you are losing clients because they believe you are overcharging them, you can lower your prices accordingly. If you find yourself without enough competing service providers to get a realistic fee estimate, be happy.

When a potential client looks out over all the personal trainers available, what will draw them to you? Not all clients will make an in-depth search for a trainer, but all will attempt to find the best match of trainer for their particular needs. Having worked hard to find your niche, you know you will not appeal to all or even a majority of clients seeking services. That is all right; you do not want to work with everyone needing fitness and exercise services. You only need to find enough individuals to fill your daily planner. To do this, be observant and find what sets you apart from the competition. Your own unique points of service and expertise are your marketing positives. Use them to your best advantage.

Finally, your promotional work and advertising consists of getting the word out on your unique points. Broadcasting these points and your availability by whatever means possible is vital to growing your new business. Even if you are strained for funds, you can ask friends to talk to everyone about your new service business. You can place simple flyers in supermarkets and other public places that tell of your services and give your phone number. Simply writing your name on a piece of paper and giving it to a potential customer actually works. Talk to people at gyms and at the local mall. Wherever people congregate, you have the potential to find new clients.

One of your best sources of new clientele will be your peers. Other personal trainers who have built their practice to the point that they are not seeking new clients may refer them to you. If you have tried to maintain good relations with your peer group, you might find you have a steady stream of referrals to keep you busy. A gym where you have worked or just been a member may offer you clients as a service to their customers and as a thanks to you for your past patronage.

As part of your business plan and marketing efforts, you should have been able to focus on what your target audience will be. Below are some suggestions for reaching these clients.

Newsletters

This can be monthly, biannual, or annual in frequency, or just one you send out to explain who you are and what you do. It can contain facts about fitness and health and the benefits of having a personal trainer.

If you have a regular newsletter, you can focus on different aspects as they relate to services you offer, such as upper-body sculpting; working areas such as abs, hips, and waist; or how to tighten your buttocks.

A newsletter differs from a brochure in that it offers information and tips rather than just information about your business. You can send these newsletters to potential or new clients. The information contained in this newsletter will be helpful and give suggestions on different aspects of health and fitness that you offer that the client may not have considered. It is important that when you are discussing an aspect of your services, you include your fees and contact information.

Here is a list of desktop publishing programs you may want to use and their average prices:

Y Art Explosion Publisher Pro — $90

Y Page Plus — $30

- ⵉ Print Shop Pro Publisher — $95

- ⵉ Microsoft Office Publisher — $99

- ⵉ Print Shop — $45

- ⵉ Print Shop Essentials — $20

- ⵉ Publishing Studio — $100

- ⵉ Design & Print — $40

- ⵉ Print Workshop — $20

More expensive does not mean better. Make sure that you are printing on quality paper and using a decent printer. Otherwise, have it printed by a professional, such as Kinko's. You need to consider the cost of printer ink, paper, and your time when making your decision.

Try to keep your newsletter to two to four pages. You can use the front and back to save money on paper and postage. Make it bright and eye-catching. Make sure your information is easy to find. If you do not have time, you can seek out a freelancer from Elance.com or Guru.com to do it for you. This will cost $200 or more, depending how elaborate you want it.

Brochures

Brochures are relatively inexpensive, especially if you get them printed in large quantities. They should be strategically placed where the clients you have targeted will frequent: doctor's offices, health food stores, vitamin stores, or gyms. On the brochure will be your company name and logo (we will discuss your logo later). You can have a picture on the front, but it should be of a healthy, fit person working out. This person should look like he or she is working hard and are benefiting from it. Your own picture does not belong on the front. Inside should be the following information:

Y What services you offer

Y The cost of the basic services

Y Positive comments from satisfied clients

On the last page, you may include a picture of yourself, and you should include all your contact information there. A simple brochure can be trifolded, giving you six panels to work with. This style also fits nicely into an envelope. You can create your own brochure and use your equipment at home. Make sure you use a good printer and paper. If it looks cheap, people will not take you seriously. You can have it designed by a freelancer if you wish. You should also consider having it printed professionally.

Your brochure is one of the strongest, most important marketing tools you will have at your disposal. It should represent everything you and your company stand for. Make sure you distribute them as many places as you can. When you are at a gym working out, make an offer to the gym owners to send business their way if they will allow you to display your brochure, or at least your business card. You can buy small holders at an office supply store. This keeps them neat and adds a touch of professionalism.

Consider having a company logo for the head of your newsletter. Unless you are an artist, it is recommended that you have a professional create a logo for you. This symbol will go on everything that you do. It represents who you are and what you do.

Do not use clip art or something you find on the Internet. It is likely that another trainer is already using that artwork or it may be copyrighted. Color graphics do not always translate well to black-and-white, so it is better that you have both color and black-and-white versions. You should also have different sizes of it made for you. When you try to shrink or enlarge a graphic, you sometimes lose the clarity of it.

The logo should represent you, the company, your tastes, and the message you are trying to convey. Spend some time and think about it before you have it made.

Blogs

Blogs are the newest way to talk to people. There are sites that cater to certain types of blogs, or you can place your blog in certain categories.

Once you get the hang of it, writing a few paragraphs every day or every few days can be done quickly. In this venue, you can talk about trials and successes and give people advice about what works in fitness and body sculpting. Just make sure you are always advertising your services and describing how you can help clients achieve the level of fitness they have always wanted. Explain how your services can take the guesswork out of fitness and allow them to concentrate on exercise rather than trying to figure out how many reps they should be doing. You can talk about trends and help the businesses you work with by mentioning them and their services. If your gyms and other vendors have a blog, ask them to return the favor.

Millions of people are reading blogs, and the numbers increase daily; use this free venue. (Some sites will charge a small fee to blog using their service.) Here are some services to consider using:

- **Y Blogger — www.blogger.com.** This is a service owned by Google. You can set up your blog free or, for more exposure, pay a fee. This is one of the most popular blog sites.

- **Y Typepad — www.typepad.com.** This popular site charges a fee after their free trial.

- **Y Bravenet — www.bravenet.com.** A popular, free blog site.

- **Y Myspace — myspace.com.** This is a place you can have your own Web page and blog. There are many young people frequenting here, but it is still a good place to put a blog.

If you have a Web site, you can also blog there or have a link from your Web site to a blog you have with another service. People do read these, so the effort is worth it.

Magazines & Newspapers

You should invest your advertising dollars in large magazines like *Fitness, Men's Health, Shape,* or *Muscle & Fitness.* The cost for magazines is much higher than in the local newspaper, although large publications, such as the *New York Times,* can be cost prohibitive. Your ad would be lost in this kind of periodical, so it is not the best use of your resources.

If you are going to advertise in a magazine, consider buying a package of advertisements. You can get a better rate and you will generate more interest among readers if they see your ad more than once. You can create the ad yourself using a desktop program, or you can hire a freelancer from Web sites such as **Elance.com** or **Guru.com**.

Mass E-mails

You can use different services online that will give you lists of e-mails to send advertisements to. This costs money, but could be worth the investment. Look for companies that will offer e-mail lists according to certain demographics such as location, age, and personal trainer interests. In your e-mail, explain your service and how to contact you. Many servers will bounce these e-mails if they are not formatted correctly. Software programs, such as the one found on **www.icontact. com**, can help.

Web Sites

If you wish to expand your business and get your name out there, you should consider setting up a Web site. This is especially important if you chose to add the sale of health products, such as nutritional supplements, to your business.

One of the largest expenses that many personal trainers pay for is setting up a Web site. There are many types of Web sites to choose from. Since personal training is service-oriented, it should contain facts about your business, packages, prices, and contact information. You may even consider having a link to send you an e-mail for more information.

Within your site, you can have galleries displaying training sessions of clients or competitions that you or clients were in. This can be a good advertising tool.

Your Web site can look much like an online version of your brochure or flyer. You can buy programs, such as FrontPage, to help you build one. This can be easy or difficult. There are many books available that can help you build a simple Web site.

The next question is where to you build your site. There are many options. There are sites that will host your Web site for free. Look at **www.free-webhosts.com** for a list of sites. The problem with this type of Web host is that they can be filled with advertisements that will be placed on your site or will have pop-up ads attached. This is a good option to start with on a limited budget.

There are sites where you must pay a monthly or yearly fee for hosting your Web site. There are large ones, such as yahoo.com and many lesser-known ones. Do your research. Some will allow you to use your own domain name, and some require that you use their Web site as part of your web address.

Some of these Web hosting services have simple programs to help you develop your site, either off or online, and will give you instructions on how to place your Web pages online. The next thing to consider is how to drive business to your Web site.

You can have another site mention your site. Another good way to drive people to your site is to make sure the Web site is on your brochures, newsletters, and business cards. You can write simple articles online and have a link to your Web site. There are many different article-posting sites. When people read your article, they will be directed to visit your Web site.

Mass e-mails that are sent out to advertise your site, should have your Web site linked within the text so that if people are interested in your services, they can read about them at their leisure. Also, join different groups and message boards relating to personal training and join in the discussion. You can then direct people to your site.

A home page is the first thing people see when they come to your Web site. First impressions are important here. It should be pleasing to the eye and easily direct the user to the different areas on your site, such as galleries, pricing, your bio, and any other pages you have chosen. If it is hard to navigate or see, you will lose people's interest and possibly lose a potential sale. Keep it simple. Do not put many graphics on your home page, as this can slow down the loading time, and people may not wait for it to load.

You should also consider making your Web site search-engine friendly. There are two main ways services such as Google will pick up your page. The first is that you pay a fee to have your Web site displayed when certain key words are entered in a search. This can be costly.

The other way is to make your Web site search engine optimized. This has to do with the way words are displayed on your Web pages. You should have certain key words and phrases on your pages in order for a search engine to choose your Web site to display. This can take much work and an understanding of the Web. There are professionals who are experts in optimizing your Web site. They can be expensive, but they will make sure your site is picked up on Google and other search engines more often.

If you choose to try to optimize your site yourself, two sites that can help you are Submit It! and Scrub The Web. There are also programs that you can buy, such as Web Position Gold that will help you optimize your site.

You need to decide for yourself if creating your own Web site fits within your schedule and abilities. Are you computer savvy enough to create an eye-popping Web site? Most personal trainers have other things to worry about besides sitting in front of a computer using programs they may not be familiar with. That is not to say a good Web site is not important; it can just be time consuming.

If you have the skills and the time, you can save money. Something to consider is what happens when your business grows. What is your plan to have your Web site grow with it? Some Web designers have packages in which they will do updates for you for a fee.

Business Cards

Spend the money to buy good stationery and business cards. Do not waste your time printing them on a printer. Nothing screams cheap and unprofessional like homemade business cards.

That does not mean you have to spend a fortune having business cards made. You can have 100 cards printed for about $10. Have them printed on good, heavy stock paper. You are trying to win people over with your style and panache. It begins with your business card.

Having good stationery is important. You will be sending out thank you cards and letters to vendors and clients often.

Having stationery made of good stock paper with your logo and information is classy.

Your business card should have the logo and business name prominently displayed. The contact information and your name should be in smaller type. Pick a color that is easy on the eye. If you choose a background, make it simple. The more things you put on a card, the harder it will be to read.

CREDENTIALING

A final point of discussion is the question of whether or not you should choose to become credentialed as a personal trainer. Only a few ordinances across the country require credentialing as a personal trainer. Additionally, numerous organizations, agencies, and businesses have set themselves up as credentialing authorities. What standards can a person use in order to choose between these organizations? Most of the personal trainers that I talked to in the case studies at the end of this book are credentialed.

Pros and Cons for Acquiring Credentials

Credentials quickly establish a level of credibility for an unknown individual. With instant credibility, your job of selling yourself and your services becomes easier. Your credentials tell the world that you possess at least a basic level of expertise.

Be aware, however, that some credentials are granted by organizations with little or no expertise in the field of personal training. They simply ask for a small fee and return mail brings you an official-looking piece of paper stating you are a qualified professional. In fact, almost anyone with a home computer can design and print official-looking credentials for themselves. Among those who choose to secure certification with the best of these organizations, there are those who have been awarded multiple certification levels; enough levels to render the individual certificates almost meaningless.

You must make your own choice as to certification. It may improve your chances of employment. Some potential employers could require some type of certification. In this case, you will be forced to seek certification. But, when you are offering your services as an individual, your clients will likely care more for your established reputation than for any paperwork. Here is where hard work and experience pays.

Perhaps the most telling argument for or against certification is the fact that the value of the certification process is used to acquire instant prestige for the practitioner from potential clients who have no prior knowledge of your services. For a new business, this certification may have value, but for established professionals, it will mean little, as clients will already be seeking you based on your reputation. Therefore, only a new practitioner would need to pursue certification.

Question your peers as to the best course of action regarding certification. Those who have been working in the field for some time will advise you as to the value of certification.

Here is a list of some places you can look at if you choose to become credentialed:

National Council on Strength and Fitness
www.ncsf.org

International Sports Sciences Association
www.issaonline.com

American Council on Exercise
www.acefitness.org

National Personal Training Institute
www.nationalpersonaltraininginstitute.com

National Academy of Sports Medicine
www.nasm.org

American College of Sports Medicine
www.acsm.org

National Council on Strength and Fitness
www.ncsf.org

National Federation of Professional Trainers
www.nfpt.com

National Exercise and Sports Trainers Association
www.nestacertified.com

Aerobics and Fitness Association of America
www.afaa.com

I would also like to suggest the site **www.starting-a-personal-training-business.com**, as it does a comparison of the different certification programs to help you choose the right one for you.

As this chapter closes, you should be able to identify your strong points and have a basic understanding of how to best promote yourself through use of these unique strengths. Entering the personal trainer field does entail much work, but it is work you can handle. In the next chapter, we will examine the various types of business models and determine which best suits your ambitions.

Tip

Make sure that you do a proper warmup and cooldown during your exercise routine. This is important for your muscles and will increase flexibility.

Business Basics 101

4

We are fast approaching the time to choose a name for your business and determine what type of business model to establish. These next steps will guide you.

WHAT IS IN A NAME?

You are choosing a name for your new baby. Sound a little over-dramatic? Consider this: Your new business will have its own identity, a tax number, and address, the same as a living being does. Incorporation of a business means that, among other things, that entity assumes its own liabilities and debts. A growing business takes on a life of its own. When several people work for the company, it has a unique personality. In addition, when a business ceases, we often say that business entity has died. We even tell others we have become a slave to our business when it drives us to work overtime and consumes more of our life than we originally chose to commit.

The name of your business, like that of a person, represents the first impression others perceive of the entity. This initial identification received by your potential customers can be extremely important to your future financial well-being. If you operate in an area where competition is fierce, the name or your enterprise may make or break your chances of acquiring new clients. If people believe that they will be comfortable working with you, based upon your business's name, they will commit to talking further with you. If they perceive a threat or something else uncomfortable about the name, you will never even know they had considered your services at all.

The business name also gives an indication of what you have to offer your clients. If you have a "hard" name, such as Get Crackin" Exercises, people will expect you to be a hard taskmaster. A soft name, such as Strolling to Good Health, will catch those individuals wanting to invest little effort.

Your business name acts as a sort of informal slogan. A name like Sassy Exercises or Jim's Bust-Out Exercising will lead to distinct expectations. Not only do these names relate to your services, they are a very basic form of marketing. A catchy name that accurately describes your offerings is a huge help in attracting new clients unfamiliar with you or your business. Some names can even be considered a very brief mission statement for that business, such as Ben's Complete Health Stop.

Try this simple brainstorming process to generate a few good candidates. Start with a large sheet of blank paper. At the top, write "Personal Trainer," and directly under that, place your name. This is what your business is all about. All potential names should lead back to this central theme. Draw a line vertically down the middle of the page. Starting on the right-hand side, list all the services you will be providing. Be complete and list any services you may be providing in the future. List everything, including the types of exercises and benefits your clientele will derive from those bodybuilding drills.

When you have exhausted your memory, use a thesaurus or a synonym finder to add alternatives to the words you have written. Once you believe you have thoroughly exhausted this services section, move on to the left-hand section.

On the left, write every descriptive term you can imagine relating to your services. Some that come immediately to mind are sweat, hard, strain, appealing, buff, and work. There are a huge variety of terms and feelings related to training. Fill this list with those emotions you find running through your head when you exercise — love, hate, distaste. Work with the thesaurus when you finish exhausting your mind again. There are many good sources on the Internet offering both a thesaurus and a synonym finder. Many of the best names come from wording found outside your own imagination.

Now that you have an extensive list of words describing your new business, take a few moments to consider a few questions that will help you to make this formidable listing more manageable. How do you view your new business in terms of what you hope to accomplish for others? What services do you really offer? You may be literally offering to physically work your clients, but you are indirectly offering them better looks, health, and longevity. What else will a potential client derive from your training services? How would you like clients to describe your services? What would you like to hear client tell their friends about their experience with you?

In a manner of speaking, the name you choose will be one stranger talking to another. Even though you do not know who will be reading your business's name, you want to make the best possible impression in that brief moment of initial contact. Naming your company is your first marketing step, and is perhaps the most important marketing move you will make. The company name should be a friendly "hello" and a warm handshake. That is not easy to do in a few simple words. Nevertheless, it is what you are striving to do right now.

Once you have considered these questions, begin to pair the words on your list. On another blank sheet of paper, put words together from the left- and right-hand columns. Take the words as they pair themselves in your mind: hurt muscles, feel push-ups, relax fitness, and free walking are a few examples. These two-word phrases will likely not be the name, but they are a springboard for your imagination. As the word pairs start to form, you will find other combinations jumping out at you. Perhaps they will cause pictures to form in your mind derived from the odd pairings.

At this moment, do not limit your creativity with thoughts of creating a meaningful phrase; that will come in its own time. Try to keep the wording simple and the words you listed originally will keep it meaningful. It is also best to use positive words and connotations.

After a few minutes, you will have a list of word pairs that appeal to you. You can start to "flesh-out" the word pairs with additional wording if you choose, but remember to keep it brief. You can add your own name to any combination of descriptive words. Many words will seem to fit better together than other alternatives. Some will rhyme and some will simply "fit."

Work in this manner until you find a few phrases that appeal to you. Unless you have one potential name that you want above all others, take the list of potentials and work with some family members or friends. Read them the list and ask them to read it back to you. Ask them to pick their favorite from among those listed and why they chose that one. This feedback is vital to your name quest. What may be the winner to you may hold little appeal to others. You should like the name of your business, but you are not the one who will be purchasing the services.

Once you have made a final choice, look carefully at the words one more time. Is it a positive, easily pronounceable name? Does it accurately reflect your business? If it feels good and rolls off your tongue easily, you have made your name choice.

Now you must be sure that your new business name is not registered by another company. In general, you will only be competing for names against companies listed in your state. For a quick check, you can do a search on the Internet. These online searches will quickly turn up any challengers or duplications, but they are not exhaustive.

Virtually all states now have an online searchable database where you can do a trade name or trademark search. This will quickly tell you whether your name is available in your state. Federal authorities will normally recognize a name registered in any state, with few exceptions.

If you cannot find access to your state's trade name database online or have other problems with this issue, contact your state senator or representative. Their secretary can do a quick search for you. There are also online services available that will research your proposed name for you. These companies charge a nominal fee for such a search. One such offering is from the organization Tradename.com at **www.tradename.com**. They will do a name search for $80.

Now you can move on to the next trial for your potential name. As a prerequisite to doing business, you will need to secure a federal Employer Identification Number (EIN) from the IRS, using IRS Form SS-4. The form can be downloaded online and, after completing it, returned to the IRS. This can also be accomplished by making application online at **www.irs.gov/pub/irs-pdf/fss4.pdf** A complete discussion about the application for small business is found at **www.irs.gov/businesses/small/article/0,,id=102767,00.html**. This form and all other federal forms are generally available or can be ordered through your local post office. Once you have made the application, you will be notified of whether or not it is accepted.

When you choose a name, you may want to register and trademark it. You will register it as a DBA. This will allow your company to exist as a separate entity from you. This is necessary if you form an LLC, but is a good idea to do even as a sole proprietor. Different states have rules and forms to do this. A good place to go is **www.dbaform.com**. Some banks will require this before you can open an account using your business name. Here is a sample statement:

STATEMENT OF INTENTION TO CONDUCT BUSINESS UNDER AN ASSUMED OR FICTITIOUS NAME

The undersigned party does hereby state his/her intention to carry on the business of _____ at the business location of _____ , in the City of _____, in the State of _____ , under the assumed or fictitious name of: _____
_____ .

STATEMENT OF INTENTION TO CONDUCT BUSINESS UNDER AN ASSUMED OR FICTITIOUS NAME

The owner's name, home address, and percentage of ownership of the above-named business are as follows:

Name: _____

Address _____

Percentage of Ownership: 100 percent

Signed on _____ , 20 _____.

_____

Business Owner Signature

_____

Business Owner Printed Name

You can chose to trademark your name, but this is not as necessary as a DBA. You can find the necessary forms and information at **www.uspto.gov.**

Should there be a duplicate name, you will have to alter your name choice. If your state requires you to submit sales tax returns, and it likely will, this will also check whether another business is claiming your chosen name. Once you have registered your name choice with state and federal agencies, you will enjoy an exclusive right of use for it. It may appear to be difficult to find a unique name, but there are millions of possible word combinations available.

You have now secured your business name and are ready to take the next step. What form of business will you be using? You can start this decision process by understanding what you wish to accomplish for yourself by establishing your business in the first place. Do you want to employ only yourself as a personal trainer? Do you want to employ others to provide services for your company? How many employees do you anticipate having? How about other employees, such as a secretary and bookkeeper? These are a few of the questions that will drive the decision of what form your business will take.

Fortunately, you can change the business format as you grow. For example, you can start with a simple sole proprietorship and then incorporate your business as it expands — if you choose to expand. For the moment, let us briefly discuss the various forms your business can take.

SOLE PROPRIETOR

A business held by a single individual and operated as an extension of that individual is a sole proprietorship. This business model is simply you announcing to the world that you are doing business as the name you have chosen for your personal trainer business. A sole proprietor business is a convenient means of tracking business expenses for tax purposes. It is a means of differentiating your personal life from your business life.

Sole proprietorship means that all profits of the company are the property of the owner, as are all debts, taxes, and other liabilities of the company. The sole proprietor business model uses a simple accounting system as the owner keeps the records in their own name. Registration of the business as a sole proprietorship allows the owner to open a business account with banking institutions.

This type of business is advantageous because decisions can be made quickly; administration is by the owner, designated employees, or family members. The tax returns for a sole proprietorship consist of only two extra pages and other government regulations are minimal. Compared to other types of business structures, a sole proprietorship faces the least amount of governmental regulation.

Disadvantages for a sole proprietorship include unlimited liability for the owner, limited ability to raise capital, and less sense of legitimacy. The owner is responsible for all liabilities of the business from whatever source. This unlimited liability is a point that forces many owners to incorporate. The raising of capital is restricted to the owner's own ability and credit. As the business has no assets of its own, the owner must provide personal collateral for any loans. The world is going to view your business as simply an extension of yourself. This type of business, for better or worse, is not a freestanding entity as is an incorporated business. It will always be viewed as you with another name.

PARTNERSHIPS

A partnership type of business format is one in which there are two or more partners sharing in the business. For example, if you and a friend, who also happens to be a personal trainer, decide to form a small business to share bookkeeping and other business overhead expenses, you would be forming a partnership. A partnership can be set up in many ways.

Partners bring certain assets and other properties of value to the partnership. If all partners provide an equal amount of value, they will likely share equally in the profits derived from the partnership. From this basic type of partnership springs the limited partnership (LP), limited liability partnership (LLP), and limited liability limited partnership (LLLP). Within these more complex types of business relationships are found both limited partnerships (LP) and general partnerships (GP).

General Partnership (GP)

Small partnerships generally have all partners sharing equally. This most basic form of business arrangement between two or more partners is known as a GP. A GP is often used to avoid the double taxation found in C-type corporations (more about incorporation later in this chapter). The partners are liable for all debts and taxes of the partnership. In a general partnership, any partner can obligate the business for loans and other debts.

Most partnerships have some form of written agreement between the partners simply to reduce friction between the individuals. Partnerships are often difficult to maintain due to the friction that develops when one partner feels they are contributing more than others and should be rewarded accordingly. These bad feelings can often be avoided by having a written agreement that spells out exactly the duties and means of profit sharing for each individual partner.

Limited Partnership (LP)

When a partnership progresses to the point where there is an uneven distribution of income among partners, it becomes a type of limited partnership. In this arrangement, each partner has a predefined proportion of earnings according to an agreement with the other partners. A general partner has a full share of management control and a full share in the profits (and liabilities). A limited partner has no managerial control and only shares in profits to the point defined by their agreement.

A limited partner might be a person who provides cash or another valuable item to the business in return for a certain portion of the company income. The limited partner would have no control over the direction of the company, but would have made their investment decision voluntarily based upon their prior knowledge of the partnership. If a limited partner does take a management role, they become a general partner. Limited partners sometimes enjoy protections from the company's liabilities.

General and limited partners have varying responsibilities for reporting their status within a partnership, depending upon the state or region in which the business is located. It is a good idea to obtain legal counsel if there is any question in fulfilling your responsibilities.

Should you have an individual interested in investing in your new personal trainer venture, but they have no interest in providing services or playing an active management role in the company, they may be interested in becoming a limited partner with you. They could share a predetermined amount of the company earnings in return for their investment. An attorney would be able to write a partnership agreement that would define the relationship and whether they would be sheltered from the company's liability.

Limited Liability Company (LLC)

This type of organization is used to help shelter the owners of a company from some of the business liabilities attached to the business. Depending upon the state in which this business is registered, it may be required to register as a corporation. In other areas, the company can be a hybrid type of partnership governed by a separate set of rules, as opposed to a normal partnership or sole proprietorship. The LLC represents the best of both corporate and partnership-type business models. The LLC shelters the various partners from liabilities originating from normal business operations, while the profits are passed directly to those partners and not taxed prior to leaving the business. The LLC has only recently become a legal option in the United States, but it has been used in many countries around the world for many years.

Closely related to the LLC is the professional limited liability company (PLLC). These organizations are partnerships of professionals. Care should be taken to ensure that your career is properly identified by the state in which you reside or wish to establish your PLLC. Some states will recognize personal trainers as a profession and some will not. Refer to state statutes to determine your standing in your state prior to application as a PLLC.

An LLC is established by registering the business partnership with your state authorities, generally the State Attorney General or Secretary of State. All states now have a Web presence, and the official state site will guide you to the appropriate authority. At a minimum, you will be able to download the appropriate state forms to submit and establish your LLC. Most states now offer an online form that you can submit directly for your company and pay the established fees with a credit card.

You will have to provide Articles of Organization, sometimes called a Certification of Organization, with your application. These articles consist of all contact information for yourself and your partners, name of the company, EIN, description of the nature of the business (personal training), any dates of dissolution of the company if planned, and who is authorized to conduct business for the company. These items would be required of any individual or entity wishing to conduct business. Some kind of operating agreement negotiated among the various partner-owners is not required by law, but highly recommended.

An operating agreement spells out exact business practices and agreement as to responsibilities and privileges of all partners. Like a set of bylaws, the agreement would give specific form for all business dealings of the LLC. This agreement would define rules for profit sharing, ownership, responsibilities, and ownership changes. A thorough agreement will avert many potential arguments and lawsuits.

INCORPORATION

A corporation is a legal entity created by the owners under the authority of a state. The owners become shareholders once the corporation comes formally into existence. The corporation is then considered an entity separate from, but owned by, the shareholders. The corporation has all the rights and obligations as an individual under the law. A corporation can borrow money, enter into contracts, sue and be sued, pay taxes separately from its shareholders, and conduct all other business, as would an individual. It shelters its owners from most legal and tax liabilities.

Once formed, a corporation continues to be in existence, regardless of ownership, until the shareholders decide to dissolve the corporation, pay all liabilities, and divest the corporate assets. Corporations can be roughly divided into two main groups: privately held and public corporations.

Public corporations will have varying amounts of outstanding stock that likely will be traded publicly. A closely held corporation has few shares outstanding and few stockholders. An example of a closely held corporation could be a family farm or other business with only family members or a few close friends holding the total outstanding stock ownership for the company.

There are various types of corporations. Here we will discuss the C- and S-type corporations. The primary difference between these two is the way they deal with tax obligations. Other types of corporations outside our current consideration are municipal (towns and city governments), nonprofits (normally charitable organizations), and quasi-public corporations, which serve public needs, such as utility or telephone companies.

C Corporation

A C corporation can be considered a "full-fledged" corporation. It is a fully independent entity owned by shareholders who may or may not be involved in management or operations. Shares of the corporation represent ownership. The amount of shares owned in relation to the total shares outstanding represents your potential to influence management of the company. The larger the number of shares you own, the more likely the company managers are to pay attention to your desires.

The major problem encountered when investing in a C corporation is that the profits of the company are taxed the same as if it were an individual. Then, the profits of the corporation are passed to you as a dividend. This income through dividends is, in turn, subject to your own personal income tax. This is often referred to as "double taxation," and it can represent a considerable tax burden. If you and your family own the outstanding shares in the corporation, and are the only or primary beneficiaries of the company profits, you might lose a significant portion of the profits to taxes. There are, however, remedies for this loss.

LLCs provide many of the benefits of incorporation, while retaining the attractive benefits of a partnership or sole proprietorship. Specifically, the income of the business is taxed only once. When taxes are filed at the end of the year, they are treated as the personal income of the partners. A possible remedy for the double taxation dilemma of the C corporation is that if it is a closely held corporation and the principal shareholders are the officers of the company, profits may be paid to the officers in lieu of declaring a dividend. If the company showed no profit, there will be no taxes paid on the corporate profits, only taxes paid by the officers based on their salaries.

It is always advisable to seek assistance and guidance from qualified tax professional or a tax attorney.

S Corporation

Companies incorporated under Subchapter S of the Internal Revenue Code, called S corporations, have some attractive benefits for a personal trainer business. S corporations must have less than 100 shareholders. This type of corporation allows the profits of the business to be passed directly to the shareholders, which means that the profits are only taxed once. Another advantage of S corporations, and closely held corporations in general, is that the relatively low number of shareholders means that these companies can make and implement rapid decisions. If the company finds itself in a rapidly changing business environment, it can adapt much more rapidly than large, publicly held incorporations.

BASICS OF INCORPORATION

As you will likely be forming a small, closely held corporation, the cost and work involved will be minimal. You have chosen the company name, secured an EIN, and are now ready to file for your corporate authority. You will need to prepare some corporate documentation, as described below.

The Articles of Incorporation

The articles of incorporation describe your business to the state. Each state regulates the content requirements for incorporation, and these requirements will vary from state to state. The following information will be required:

- Complete contact information for the corporation

- Complete contact information for the incorporators

- The purpose of the corporation (a brief description of services offered)

- Voting rights of the shareholders

- A description of the share structure (what type and how many shares)

- A list of names of the original board of directors and their related contact information

- Names and contact information for initial corporate officers

- The registered agent for the corporation — this is the person who will be officially authorized to receive certain legal documentation for the company, such as notification of law suits

Y Signatures of the incorporators

Bylaws

The bylaws are the blueprint of the organization. They will describe the company and how you plan to do business. The bylaws will include the following:

Y Complete contact information for the corporate entity

Y Description of the board of directors: how they are to be chosen; how many members; length of term in office; allowance for removal of officers; what, if any, compensation they will receive; and the names and addresses of the officers

Y The number and type of shares the corporation can issue

Y Description of the protocol for meetings of shareholders, along with the frequency and location of the meetings

Y Description of the record-keeping system to be used by the company and what will happen if the bylaws are in conflict with the articles of incorporation

Y The procedure for amending both the bylaws and the articles of incorporation

Certificate of Incorporation

You will file for this document at your state Attorney General's or Secretary of State's office. Forms are available online or obtainable through a phone call to either office. Again, your state representative or senator can assist you in obtaining forms or tracking these documents through the governmental review process. Do not hesitate to ask your local elected officials for assistance. After completing the documentation, return it to the proper state agency and wait for the official documents and official corporate seal to arrive in a week or two.

Resolutions of the Board of Directors

At the first meeting of the board, members will formally accept the bylaws and all other documentation or regulation required by state law. Also approved will be initial distribution of stock certificates and other necessary financial issues, such as authorizing bank accounts and loans. Other initial business might include the following:

- Declaring officially the corporate officers, authorizing them to conduct the business of the corporation, and approving their salary and other benefits

- Adopting shareholder buy-out agreements

- Authorizing official meeting minutes, corporate forms, and other documentation; employee hiring practices and procedures, along with salary and wage benefits; authorizing officers to secure various permits and licenses in the name of the corporation; and other vital business issues

- If the board of directors elects to be an S corporation, the board must authorize the corporate officers to file notice and submit applicable documentation with the IRS.

There may be numerous licenses, permits, or other legal requirements to fulfill at your particular business location. Seek advice from your city, county, and state authorities as to complete regulations governing business establishment and the conduct of business. Your elected officials are there to help you when necessary; use their assistance.

Corporate Officers

The officers of the corporation are responsible for the day-to-day operation of the business. Under the direction of the board of directors, as specified by the corporate bylaws, the officers are appointed by the board for a specific or nonspecific term of office. The officer positions normally include:

- Ψ President or Chief Executive Officer (CEO)

- Ψ Vice-president

- Ψ Treasurer or Chief Financial Officer (CFO)

Formation of any of these types of business at the most basic level is relatively simple. There are numerous individuals, agencies, and organizations available to lend assistance. Do not hesitate to seek free advice from any of these if you encounter difficulties. It is advisable to start your business at the least complex level possible because it is always easily enlarged as you grow and expand services. The more business you have, the more resources will be available to pay experts, such as accountants and attorneys.

You have now named your business and decided upon a model in which to conduct business. In Chapter 5, you will find more in-depth detail on how to operate your new business. You have made significant progress toward your goal of opening your own personal training business.

Business Basics 102

5

OPERATING PROCEDURES

Early in your company's life span, operating procedures will primarily cover your record keeping, billing, and administrative sections. You should be able to demonstrate the ability to accurately record the services and explain exactly how you will collect for them.

You should determine a system for pricing your services. A listing of other personal trainers and their fee structures is the best means of accomplishing this. List the fees of several trainers and you could easily take the average fees charged as a starting point for your own purposes. Lack of competition or inability to learn of the competition's pricing structure means you will have to find similar communities and learn their practices. Your peers will assist you if they do not perceive you as a threat.

Collecting payment is a delicate subject. You must insist on payment for your services without alienating your clientele. Of course, if a client refuses to pay you, that client's services must be terminated. This will likely be a rare occurrence. Slow payment is a more common issue. Repeated billing should help.

After you have collected the service fees, you must account for the funds until final disbursement. This is necessary for all stakeholders in the company, as well as for tax purposes. You will need a receipt for each business-related expense. Your company records can be kept in a cardboard box, but a better impression will be made on potential lenders or investors if you have an organized system of records management.

Your records can consist of one ledger book to enter cash transactions and another to keep track of services provided. You could use a complex computerized system if you have that expertise or if the business can afford the services of someone well-versed in computerized accounting. Whatever method you choose should create a clear trail of where the money came from and where it has gone.

EVALUATING YOUR SUCCESS AFTER SIX MONTHS

One way to evaluate how your business is doing and ways to improve is to do an analysis of a analysis of your business's strengths, weaknesses, opportunities, and threats (SWOT).

The strengths and weaknesses are determined in reference to your competition and others in the industry, not based upon your own history. Strengths and weaknesses are internal to your business. Opportunities and threats are from external sources, such as your competition. These competitors are current and new arrivals on the personal training scene.

A SWOT analysis will help you focus your energy on areas where you are the strongest and identify and concentrate on greatest the opportunities.

HOW TO DO A SWOT ANALYSIS

The first thing you will consider is your business strengths. I have included a worksheet here, which can be found on the CD-ROM. Here are some things to consider as you fill out this worksheet:

Y What sets your service apart in the industry?

Y What does your business do well?

Y What resources and contacts do you have to work with?

Y What do your clients say your company's strengths are? (You can get this information by sending them an evaluation form for your service. See the next section for examples.)

When you fill your worksheet out, make sure you are honest, and do not be modest. Put items in that make your company shine.

Worksheet SWOT — Strengths

On this worksheet, make sure you are adding your company's internal strengths and what sets them apart from other personal trainer businesses. You can add as many strengths as you wish. When you are done, figure out what your top eight strengths are.

STRENGTHS

Your Company's Strengths:

1. _____

2. _____

3. _____

Description of the Strengths (Be Clear and Concise):

1. _____
_____
_____

2. _____
_____
_____

3. _____
_____
_____

Ways to Continue to Build on the Strengths:

1. _____
_____
_____

2. _____
_____
_____

3. _____
_____
_____

Worksheet SWOT — Weaknesses

The next thing you will evaluate is your company's weaknesses. Here are some questions to help you through that process:

Y What are the things that can be improved in your business?

Ŷ What does your business do less well than you would like?

Ŷ What things have your clients said need improvement in your company? (This can be drawn from comments or a survey done with them after you have completed your service with them.)

Ŷ Is your competition doing better than you are?

As with the strengths, you want to be honest. No one needs to see this list but you, so put it all out there.

On the following worksheet, list the weaknesses of your personal training business. These can be deficiencies in the resources or capabilities of your company. These are roadblocks that stop you from following your mission and values statements during the course of doing business. You may add as many weaknesses as you wish. When you are finished, figure out what your eight highest-priority weaknesses are.

WEAKNESSES
Your Company's Weaknesses
1. _____
2. _____
3. _____
Description of the Weaknesses (Be Clear and Concise):
1._____
_____
_____
2._____
_____
_____

WEAKNESSES

3. _____

_____

_____

Ways to Improve on the Weaknesses:

1. _____

_____

_____

2. _____

_____

_____

3. _____

_____

_____

Worksheet SWOT — Opportunities

As mentioned earlier, opportunities come from external sources. As you fill out your opportunities worksheet, consider using the following questions:

- Where are the best opportunities for your company?

- What are the new trends in the personal trainer and fitness personal training industry?

- Where can you find these new trends?

- Are there changes in the market that can improve your business?

- Are there new places to do business to be considered?

- Are there places to find new clients?

You can look at your strengths list and consider what and where to find the opportunities that can help you bolster your strengths. You can also look at your weaknesses list and consider where you might find ways to eliminate some of these weaknesses.

On the following worksheet, consider outside factors and people who can improve your personal trainer company. You can list as many opportunities on your sheet as you choose. When you are finished, compare them to your vision statement, value statement, and any other component in your business plan. See if they agree with each other. You may have to adjust your plan or your opportunity to make sure you are placing your focus on the right items. When you have completed your changes, come up with a plan to implement using your opportunities.

OPPORTUNITIES

Your Company's Opportunities:

1. _____

2. _____

3. _____

Description of the Opportunities (Be Clear and Concise):

1. _____

_____

_____

2. _____

_____

_____

3. _____

_____

_____

OPPORTUNITIES

Ways to Continue to Build on the Opportunities:

1._____
_____
_____

3._____
_____
_____

3._____
_____
_____

Worksheet SWOT — Threats

The last component of your SWOT analysis is threats. These are external threats and should not be confused with weaknesses. Here are some questions to help you fill out your threats worksheet:

- ϒ What obstacles does your business face?

- ϒ What is your competition doing that is affecting your company?

- ϒ Are there any regulations or laws that have changed about operating a personal trainer business?

- ϒ Is your company facing financial or debt problems?

On this worksheet, you will be listing situations, people, and factors that affect your personal training business in a negative way. You may list as many factors as you wish. Decide which factors are in your control and which are not. Come up with a plan to try to reduce or eliminate threats that you do have control over.

THREATS

Your Company's Threats:

1. _____

2. _____

3. _____

Description of the Threats (Be Clear and Concise):

1. _____
   _____
   _____

2. _____
   _____
   _____

3. _____
   _____
   _____

Ways to Continue to Minimize the Threats:

1. _____
   _____
   _____
   _____

2. _____
   _____
   _____

3. _____
   _____
   _____

SURVEYS

When you have completed work with a client, it is always nice to send them a thank you card. In it, you can add two important things to help your company. The first is some extra business cards, and the other is a short survey.

On the back of the business card, write the name of your client. That way, when a new potential client calls, you will know where the referral came from. Keep a running tally of the number of word-of-mouth referrals you get. It can help your SWOT analysis, and your marketing strategy.

The survey should be brief. It is good if you can write it on self-mailing cards so that when they are finished, all your customers have to do is send it back in the mail with the postage already paid. Keep a tally of the number of returned surveys to see whether this is a good marketing strategy for you.

Here is a sample thank you letter and a sample survey:

SAMPLE THANK YOU LETTER

Sally Brown Personal Trainers
123 Main Street
Anywhere, USA

January 18, 2008

Mr. Man in Training
456 N. Main Street
Anywhere, USA

Dear Mr. Training:

On behalf of everyone at Sally Brown Personal Trainers, thank you for choosing us to help you with your fitness needs.

We are committed to helping our clients live a healthy life style and work to get the body they want, while providing the highest level of customer satisfaction possible. If you have any questions or comments, we would be delighted to hear from you. Call us at 1-800-555-1234, or send us an e-mail at sallybrowntraining@service.com. You can expect us to respond to your e-mail within 24 hours.

SAMPLE THANK YOU LETTER

Our company relies on the generosity of you, our clients, in spreading the word about our superb fitness training services. I have included some business cards that I hope you will give to your family and friends so that we can help them with their fitness and body-sculpting needs.

In addition, I have included a quick survey. It takes less than five minutes to fill out, and you can fold it and send it back to me, as it is a self-addressed, stamped postcard. Please be honest and add any comments that we can use to improve the way we do business. If you would like to add positive comments, we would love to use them on our Web site and promotional materials.

Again, thank you for your patronage. We wish you the best of luck with your health and well-being.

Sincerely,

Sally Brown
Certified Personal Trainer

SAMPLE SURVEY

Sally Brown Personal Trainer Survey

Please fill out the following survey. Circle the number that most closely represents your answer. 1 is strongly agree, 2 is agree, 3 is no opinion, 4 is disagree, and 5 is strongly disagree. When you are finished, please fold this paper in half, with the address label and stamp on the outside, and mail it back to us. You can staple or tape the ends firmly. Thank you for your time and generosity.

1. Sally Brown paid attention to my needs and goals.
   1...2...3...4...5

2. Sally listened to my vision of my health and body image.
   1...2...3...4...5

3. Sally was always able to be reached.
   1...2...3...4...5

4. I will recommend Sally to friends and family for their fitness and training needs.
   1...2...3...4...5

SAMPLE SURVEY

5. Sally's fees were reasonable.
      1...2...3...4...5

6. Sally was knowledgeable about training, fitness, and health.
      1...2...3...4...5

7. Sally is someone I trust.
      1...2...3...4...5

8. Sally was able to provide product suggestions that helped my bodybuilding needs.
      1...2...3...4...5

9. Sally was able to meet my scheduling needs.
      1...2...3...4...5

10. Sally was sensitive to my feelings.
      1...2...3...4...5

EVALUATING YOUR SUCCESS AFTER ONE YEAR

When you reach the year mark, it is time look at where you have been, where you are, and where you want to go. If you did not already do a SWOT analysis or are ready to do another one, this is a good time to do so.

After one year, you should send out surveys to your contacts (gyms, fitness equipment providers, health product providers). These should be similar to the ones you send to clients. This provides feedback about the strengths and weaknesses of your company.

It is at the one-year mark that you have to do some honest soul searching. Does your personal training business have what it takes to succeed?

Do not use the money you are making as the only component to determine whether your business is viable. It can take a few years to get any small business to make a profit. You do want to at least break even. You may be worrying about how to keep the lights on at home. You may need to work a part-time job until your business can turn a profit.

If you are getting a steady stream of referrals and your calendar is beginning to fill up, this is a good indication of success. There are some things to consider when looking at work as a personal trainer. There are times of the year when clients will be looking for a personal trainer, so you should plan time off during the slower periods.

The two main busy times for personal trainers are in January and the beginning of summer. January is when people are trying to follow through with New Year's resolutions. They also may be looking to lose some extra pounds they gained over the holidays. The summer is when people are planning to wear bathing suits and want to look their best. Just before the holidays is another time people will be looking to lose a few pounds so they can look their best during holiday parties and gatherings.

This will vary from area to area, based upon climate, culture, current trends, and availability issues. You should keep a calendar for the year and look at when new clients may be looking for a trainer. These times can change slightly from year to year, but you should find that they follow a predictable pattern.

PERSONNEL

Include a complete listing of all employees and any board of directors or other oversight agency. The list should include the name, position, and length of employment for each individual. It

The person's place and need within the business structure should be apparent. Here you will be justifying the existence of each employee position and showing its value to the overall business.

A salary justification may or may not be demanded. If you are asked to justify a particular salary, have available information for comparable positions in the local personal trainer industry to validate your pay structure decision.

Having just started your personal trainer business, you will likely be the sole employee. This greatly reduces the personnel description and means you only will be justifying your own employment.

If you decide to hire employees, there are taxes and expenses to be considered. If your business grows to the point that you feel stretched and you have determined that your business is viable and is making a profit, you can consider hiring employees. You may need to check the laws concerning hiring in your area and state. Make sure you follow the guidelines of fair hiring practices. A good place to look for and request copies of this information is from the United States Office of Personnel Management. Here you will find the current laws and practices of hiring and maintaining employees. They can be found at **www.opm.gov.**

How can you be sure you are hiring the right person? You could hire an intern or someone who is looking to apprentice. These can be energetic, motivated college students who may be studying small business or trying to get a degree in a fitness-related field. They will want to help, in addition to making a little money. Check with your local colleges, community colleges, and business schools.

Take your time. The person you hire must be someone you trust because you will probably hire them to work independently, doing tasks that you would normally be doing. You need to feel confident that they can perform according to your standards.

Here are a few areas in which you may decide to hire personnel to help you in your personal training business:

- Y If you have an office with a few employees, you might consider an office manager who can take care of day-to-day administrative, clerical, and office supply duties.

- Y As you grow, you may need another personal trainer. This person should have experience in personal training, and be dedicated to your business. Be sure to check a number of references closely before hiring this person, as they could help or destroy your business's name and reputation.

- Y If you need someone to conduct classes, such as aerobics or martial arts, you might consider hiring a part-time or full-time teacher. This person should be creative, flexible, and good with people.

- Y If you are running a large, high-profile company, you may need to hire a public relations person to take care of talking to clients, vendors, or the general public. They must have diplomacy, communication skills, and the ability to answer questions under pressure.

- Y If you do not have time to market your company, you can hire a freelance marketing manager. This person can take care of advertising, promotion, market analysis, and company direction.

- If you want to hand over the financial aspects of your business to someone who has a love for numbers, you may consider hiring a bookkeeper. This should be someone with some education and experience. A retired bookkeeper who is looking for some part-time work may be your best option.

- If you like making a mess, but not cleaning it up, you may consider hiring a cleaning service. This person helps clean your area and the machines you use. It is important that they sanitize all of the equipment. If you run a gym, you may also want to hire a laundry service.

- If you would like someone to help greet people when they come in and help to schedule times and give out towels, you should hire a person to work at the front desk. This person should be good at directing people and answering questions, and should be someone that you trust implicitly.

- If you want to get into the health product vendor side of things, you may want to contract with a company or two to sell their products. If you want to make your own products, this is a big undertaking, as you would need to set up a kitchen or have someone help you. It can improve your profits, but it can entail much more work.

- You may need to contract with fitness equipment suppliers. Even if you have your own equipment to start, it will eventually wear out or become obsolete.

These are just some of the people you may want or need to hire. Some of these jobs can be combined, as one job may not offer enough hours for someone to commit to working for you. Once you have decided to hire the person, you may want them to sign a contract, in addition to having them fill out W-4 and state tax forms.

GENERAL EMPLOYMENT CONTRACT

This Contract is made on _____ , 20 ____ , between _____ _____, Employer, of _____ , City of _____ ____, State of _____ , and _____ , Employee, of _____ , City of _____ , State of _____ ____.

In order for both parties to work together as a team, the Employer and Employee agree as follows:

1. The Employee agrees to perform the following duties and job description: _____ _____

(Write down every aspect of the job the person is to do. If you add items later, it should be added on this form and initialed or a new form should be created.)

This is considered a full-time/part-time position.

2. The Employee will begin work on _____ , 20 ____. This position shall continue for a period of _____ . (Either a time frame or a specific date.)

3. The Employee will be paid the following: _____

Weekly salary (this also may be hourly or monthly): _____

The Employee will also be given the following benefits: (This may not be applicable, but make sure that you follow state and federal guidelines.)

Sick Pay: $_____

Vacations: _____

GENERAL EMPLOYMENT CONTRACT

Bonuses: _____

Retirement Benefits: _____

Insurance Benefits: _____

4. The Employee agrees to abide by all rules and regulations of the Employer at all times while employed. In addition, they will read and agree to the company's business plan, vision statement, and value statement.

5. This Contract may be terminated by:

   (a) Breach of this Contract by the Employee;

   (b) The expiration of this Contract without renewal;

   (c) Death of the employee;

   (d) Incapacitation of the Employee for more than _____ days in any one year. (You may chose to add, delete, or modify anything you choose in this section.)

6. The Employee agrees to sign the following additional documents as a condition to obtaining employment: (You can add other documents, such as a non compete agreement and an agreement not to divulge anything about the company and how it operates to any outside entity.)

7. Any dispute between the Employer and Employee related to this Contract will be settled by voluntary mediation. If mediation is unsuccessful, the dispute will be settled by binding arbitration using an arbitrator of the American Arbitration Association. (This professional organization can help settle disputes outside of court for a fee. For more information, visit **www.adr.org**)

8. Any additional terms of this Contract:

9. No modification of this Contract will be effective unless it is in writing and is signed by both the Employer and Employee. This Contract binds and benefits both parties and any successors. Time is of the essence of this Contract. This document is the entire agreement between the parties. This Contract is governed by the laws of the State of _____.

GENERAL EMPLOYMENT CONTRACT

Dated: _____

_____

Signature of Employer

_____

Printed name of Employer

_____

Signature of Employee

_____

Printed name of Employee

(You may want to have a notary notarize your agreement.)

You also want to have a written contract with independent contractors who work for you, such as class instructors. For instance, a class on nutrition is a short-term engagement that does not require you to hire the person as an employee. A signed contract can save you money, time, and aggravation. If you have to take a subcontractor to court, a signed contract can be the document to tip the scales in your favor.

INDEPENDENT CONTRACTOR AGREEMENT

This Agreement is made on _____, 20 ___ , between_____ _____, Company (your personal training business), of _____, City of _____, State of _____, and _____, Vendor, of _____, City of _____, State of _____.

1. The Independent Contractor, agrees to furnish all of the labor and materials to do the following portions of the work specified in the Agreement between the Company and the Contractor dated _____, 20 ____

INDEPENDENT CONTRACTOR AGREEMENT

2. The Independent Contractor agrees that the following portions of the total work will be completed by the dates specified:

Work: _____

Dates: _____

3. The Independent Contractor agrees to perform this work in a professional manner, according to standard practices in their industry. If any plans or specifications are part of this job, they are attached and are part of this Contract.

4. The (Company) agrees to pay the Independent Contractor as full payment $ _____ for doing the work outlined above. This price will be paid to the Independent Contractor upon satisfactory completion of the work in the following manner and on the following dates:

Work: _____

Dates: _____

5. Company and Independent Contractor may agree to extra services and work, but any such extras must be set out and agreed to in writing by both the Company and the Independent Contractor.

6. The Independent Contractor agrees to indemnify and hold the Contractor harmless from any claims or liability arising from the Vendor's work under this Agreement.

7. No modification of this Agreement will be effective unless it is in writing and is signed by both parties. This Agreement binds and benefits both parties and any successors. Time is of the essence of this Agreement. This document, including any attachments, is the entire agreement between the parties. This Agreement is governed by the laws of the State of _____.

Dated: _____

_____

Signature of Company

INDEPENDENT CONTRACTOR AGREEMENT

Name of Company

Signature of Independent Contractor

Name of Independent Contractor

(You may want to have a Notary to sign and seal this agreement.)

The next few sections listed here should be a part of your business plan before you begin to hire employees. It helps you and the person you hire to know what is expected of them, what the structure of the company is, and what the management structure will be.

Next, we will continue with the management summary part of your business plan. You will only need this if you plan to hire employees.

MANAGEMENT SUMMARY

This section deals with the structure of your company. You will list what type of company — sole proprietorship, partnership, or other — you have set up. After that, you will discuss who the owners are and what the actual management structure is. You can include a chart that illustrates the management system and the order of management, from the employee right up to the owners. This chart helps people know who they are responsible for, what they are responsible for, and what the chain of command is. This can change over time as positions are added, combined, or removed.

In this section, you will explain why you need the employees and what is the overall plan of paying for and supporting certain positions in the company. Included in this section is a listing of the owners and managers, and a description of their qualifications and education. This justifies the management choices and who is an expert in different aspects of the company.

PERSONNEL PLAN

In this section, you will break down the financial burden of the employees in the company. This includes how you plan to pay yourself. You should also consider what the projected cost would be to be able to hire new employees.

PERSONNEL PLAN			
	FY 2007	FY 2008	FY 2009
Owner	$53,100	$76,200	$85,800
Other	$0	$0	$20,000
Total Payroll	$53,100	$76,200	$105,800

INSURANCE

All insurance pertaining to the business should be listed and at least a copy of the current policy included. You may only have a liability policy, or your state and local authorities may demand you acquire bonding or differing types of malpractice policies. All documentation showing that you comply with all laws and ordinances should be included. If you are covered by some other entity, such as a gym, show that coverage. Any type of umbrella policy provided by another organization that covers your liability obligations should be fully documented. If you operate in a facility owned by another entity, ask whether you are covered under their insurance policy. Any lender will require you show that you will not be financially devastated should you be sued for negligence or malpractice. I will discuss various types of liability insurance and options in Chapter 7.

FINANCIAL INFORMATION

A plan to track your finances is vital. If you approach lenders, they will be anxious to observe planning in this area. You will need to be able to track all business-related income and expenses for tax purposes. If you have other stakeholders in the company, they will also need complete financial disclosure. Finally, you will need to assure yourself that there is accountability for all incoming and outgoing funds. You should be sure that no unnecessary expenses are encountered in the course of normal business.

Financial information will include documentation of all financial activities affecting the business operations, ownership, and other major company considerations.

The following is a partial listing of important financial instruments:

- **Loan applications** — Any applications pertaining to current loan activity

- **Capital equipment and supply list** — Complete inventory of company assets

- **Balance sheet** — An accurate rendering of the organization's current financial position

- **Break-even analysis** — A statement of exactly how many hours of services you will have to provide in order to cover your total expenses, generally expressed in a monthly format

'Y' **Pro-forma income projections (profit & loss statements)** — A snapshot of how well your business is performing

'Y' **Three-year summary** — Details the financial history of your company for the past three years (or any length of time less than three years for which you have been operating)

'Y' **Detail by month, first year** — Detailed income and expenses for the first 12 months the company operated

'Y' **Detail by quarters, second, and third years** — Detailed income and expense records for the past two years

'Y' **Assumptions upon which projections were based** — Using your most accurate historical financial information, make projections as to the future performance of your business

'Y' **Pro-forma cash flow** — This statement of cash flow incorporates anticipated loans and other obligations not yet incurred

END-OF-YEAR FINANCIAL ANALYSIS

At the end of the year, you will want to assess where your business is going. Earlier in the chapter, you looked at costs and an analysis of your financial situation. Here is a worksheet that will allow you to review how you are doing and areas where you need improvement in order to keep your business solvent.

END-OF-YEAR FINANCIAL ASSESSMENT	
What is the current financial status of your company?	
Income and Expenses	
Record what the annual expenses were for the first year in the following categories:	
Advertising expenses:	
Auto expenses:	
Cleaning and maintenance expenses:	
Dues and publications:	
Office equipment expenses:	
Business Insurance expenses:	
Legal and accounting expenses:	
Business meals and lodging:	
Miscellaneous expenses:	
Postage expenses:	
Office rent/mortgage expenses:	
Repair expenses:	
Office supplies:	
Federal unemployment taxes:	
State unemployment taxes:	
Telephone/Internet expenses:	
Utility expenses:	
Wages and commissions:	
Total:	
Record the first year's annual income from the following sources:	
Service income:	
Miscellaneous income (tips or bonuses received):	
Total:	
What types of debt do you currently have?	
Current liabilities:	
Taxes due:	
Accounts payable:	

END-OF-YEAR FINANCIAL ASSESSMENT	
Short-term loans/notes payable:	
Payroll accrued:	
Miscellaneous:	
Long-term liabilities:	
Other loans/notes payable:	
Financial needs:	
Total:	
Based on the estimated profits and losses of your company, what finances will you need to keep the company going?	
1st year:	
2nd year:	
3rd year:	
4th year:	
5th year:	
Total:	
Estimate the cash flow for the business for the next five years:	
1st year:	
2nd year:	
3rd year:	
4th year:	
5th year:	
Total:	
From what sources are the necessary funds expected to be raised?	
Cash on hand:	
Personal funds:	
Family:	
Friends:	
Conventional bank financing:	
Finance companies:	
U.S. Small Business Administration:	
Record the cost of doing business for the first year (This includes traveling, phone bills, or anything else you needed to perform your duties as a personal trainer.)	

END-OF-YEAR FINANCIAL ASSESSMENT	
Total:	
Assets and Liabilities	
What forms of credit have been used by your company?	
What is the cash flow of your company?	
What are the sources of that cash flow?	
What types of bank accounts are in place for the business and what are the current balances?	
What types of assets are currently owned by the business?	
Current assets:	
Cash in bank:	
Cash on hand:	
Accounts receivable:	
Autos/trucks:	
Equipment:	
Amount of depreciation taken on any of above:	
Fixed non-depreciable:	
Miscellaneous:	
Total:	

Once you have filled out the worksheet, look closely at the results of your analysis. Do you see any problems? What are the highlights? Are there any obvious cash flow problems? Was your income enough to cover your debts, or did you need to use your own personal finances or financial assistance from friends and family to cover your expenses?

You should do this analysis every year. The third and fifth years are the breaking points for most personal trainer businesses. These are the times when you can clearly assess both financial stability and your continued personal investment into your business.

HOW TO ASSESS SUCCESS

While it is important to look at the financial stability of your business as a milestone of success, there are other factors to consider when discussing the success of your personal trainer business.

1. Do you feel as though you are providing a necessary service to the fitness industry?

2. Does your target market have enough clients to continue to support your business now and in the future?

3. Do you have enough financial support to keep your business running for at least three more years?

4. Do you feel that you have a strong and clear business plan that can help you navigate your business and give you direction should you need help?

5. Is your support team strong, positive, and available?

6. Is your number-one priority still to provide the best service and to transform dreams into reality for your clients?

7. Have you done a good job of keeping up with records and paying taxes so you have a clear idea how your business is doing financially at any time?

8. Do you have a clear understanding of your competition — who they are, what they offer, and how they are doing — in comparison to your training business?

9. Do you have the flexibility to change when necessary in your business, especially when times become stressful?

10. Do you still love personal training as a career?

Supporting Documentation

ᵞ Tax returns for yourself and other principle owners for the last three years

ᵞ Personal financial statement

ᵞ Copy of proposed or existing lease for business operation facilities

ᵞ Copy of licenses and all other legal documents required for legal operation of the business entity

ᵞ Copy of employee documentation

ᵞ Documentation of all needed suppliers of equipment and supplies needed for continued operations

Include all information and documentation to support the information in the foregoing sections adequately. Also, include any information specifically requested by lenders or other stakeholders that have a bearing upon the business.

The business plan is intended to give a quick, accurate picture of the business as it exists, and an educated estimate of the near future. If you are requesting loans, include those funds and repayment options in your projections to show that the business will be capable of handling the necessary repayments. Consider the business plan as a valuable instrument for furthering the best interests of your company.

Tip

Your body adjusts to new routines quickly. Make sure that you break the pattern so that you can still get results and work your body.

Advanced Business Practices

In this chapter, you will learn about more involved business practices that may take more time and can evolve over time. These issues do not need to be resolved before you begin your business, but should be considered as your business grows.

MISSION STATEMENT

"To improve and extend the lives of our friends."

A mission statement is focus. It defines the business for both the public and yourself. The mission statement tells the world the exact purpose of your business. It is the reason for which your enterprise was established. A short, concise statement, it should contain information delivered with a punch. This statement conveys your product and an allusion to the result for the client — good health, long life, better looks, and more.

"We are working toward the enhancement and enjoyment of life."

When seeking the words for your statement, play with the wording of the services you deliver. Work with describing what you believe your clientele seeks through your working sessions. Why do they put up with the work, sweat, and pain? What could possibly be worth paying someone to abuse them with physical exercises? Perhaps it is physical allure, creating a new self-image, or simply attempting to feel better every day.

"Work hard now — live better, longer afterward."

The mission statement should create a vivid image of your service and what a potential client will take away from their sessions.

"Fitness means life, looks, and happiness."

The above examples are simple one-liners. Your mission statement may be two or more sentences, but the longer the statement, the less likely people will read to the end. A short sentence that conveys, at a glance, the total image you wish to impart is much better. If you find your mission statement approaching three or more sentences, consider distilling it down. Remove extra words and try to use one powerful word in place of several descriptors.

"We want you to live much longer and enjoy all of those extra days," can be replaced with, "Long life and sunny days." It is amazing how short a span of time you will hold the attention of potential clients. If you work in space located in a busy mall, you are competing for their attention with all the other stores surrounding you, and your services are less appealing than the cappuccino and cake next door.

If you offer weight-reduction services, your potential clients have already decided they want to improve their life through the loss of extra pounds. Your statement simply tells them that this is the place and time to do what they already want to do. You will not be able to change a complete mindset held by strangers, but you can influence those already prepared to alter their life. You can tell them they have arrived at the exact place to do that which they have already decided to attempt.

"We offer sweat equity in life."

PRICING SERVICES

How will you price your services? Averaging the price of the competition is the preferred method. If you are fortunate enough to have isolated a niche market with no competition whatsoever, your pricing is entirely up to you and your potential clients. Keep in mind that people are only going to allocate what they deem a fair price for your services, so you may find it necessary to negotiate a bit with each client. In this case, you will need to know the minimum price you can accept for your services.

When deciding upon an hourly selling price, you must understand your own personal break-even analysis. This is the point before which you cover your expenses, and after which, you realize a profit. Any price below your break-even point will result in a loss of money for you. In order to arrive at a break-even point, you will have to identify your total living costs and the cost of providing your product.

There are two basic types of expenses that you encounter: fixed and variable. A fixed cost is one that remains the same over a period. Fixed costs can be monthly rents, monthly payments, and even the base service charge portion of a utility bill. Fixed costs are constant. Variable costs are constantly changing. An electric bill will vary from month to month, depending upon the use of electricity in a particular facility.

Variable costs can become intertwined with fixed costs. This becomes a complex situation if you have to break down the electric bill into fixed monthly service charges and the portion dependant upon variable usage. Fortunately, you will be able to average a few months' or a year's worth of electric bills to arrive at a good working number to use as an expense item.

To determine your break-even point, you will need to know both your total monthly personal living expenses and the total business expense for providing your services. The total of these two will be your break-even point. This is the cost of doing business. If you have any variable expenses that will increase in relation to the total amount of services you provide, you must also consider these costs. For example, if you have a gym in which you provide personal training services, you will encounter higher electrical, water, and other expenses the more hours you use the facility. Maintenance and repair costs also increase with increased usage. If you have been in business, you will have an accurate idea of these costs. On the other hand, if you are just establishing your company, you will need to make an estimate of these costs.

To arrive at the basic break-even costs, total your entire cost of living for yourself and your family. Include all costs for which you are responsible. Arrive at a monthly average dollar figure. To this cost, add your monthly average cost of personal training services. The breakdown should look something like this:

Total personal living expense	$1,500
Total basic cost of providing services	$2,500
Total costs	$4,000

(Sums are for example use only; your costs will vary.)

Divide this number by the number of hours you will be providing services per month. Considering there are about 2080 working hours annually, divide the 2080 by 12 months, which rounds off to 173. This number is divided into the $4000 cost figure above (4000/173 = 21.12). This $21.12 figure is your base break-even amount. Added to this base figure are the estimated variable costs of providing services. Your personal living expenses are constant for this example.

If you estimate that increasing usage of your facility will increase your costs by approximately $2.50 per hour, you must add this to the break-even price of providing services. Included in this increase estimate is the use of electricity (e.g., lights and air conditioning/heating) and additional water (e.g., fountains and showers), along with any other rising costs such as linen services. These services are as much a cost of doing business as the fixed costs, and you must pay both fixed and variable costs in order to remain in business. Therefore, add your $21.12 and your $2.50 to arrive at $23.62 as a total break-even price for your services.

If you provide 173 hours of services per month, $23.62 is your hypothetical break-even price. Providing less hours will result in a higher break-even price per hour due to spreading the total costs over a smaller number of hours. Providing services for half the 173 projected service hours, or 86.5 hours, will result in a doubling of the break-even cost of those hours to $41.24. Likewise, an increase in hours of services provided over the projected 173 will reduce the break-even price.

As can be seen from this simplified example, figuring a price to charge for your services can quickly become complex. Having historical numbers to use for these figures is a huge advantage. You can even use estimates from a former employer or peers. Anything that is based in fact will be preferable to your own estimates. You will need some figure, so even one based on a "best guess" is preferable to no estimate at all. The break-even cost can be adjusted once actual expenses are established by the business.

This break-even analysis also highlights one of the primary barriers to entry into your own business: You must provide for your total expenses whether you have customers or not. The base figure of $4000 must be paid in order for you to remain a viable business entity. If you only provide one hour of services monthly, it is unlikely anyone will pay you $4000 to cover your total costs. Therefore, you must either be very effective in marketing and fill your entire 173 hours with personal training or have sufficient funds available to cover expenses until your business clientele reaches capacity.

A ray of hope here is that when you provide services and are repaid at an amount above the break-even cost, you have made a profit. If you provide your weight-loss reduction services for $30 per hour and your break-even cost is $23.62, you have realized a profit of $6.38 for that hour of work. Should you fall short of providing 173 total hours per month of services provided, the profit can be used to offset the expenses not covered by the services provided. Providing 150 hours of services at $30 per hour yields a total of $4500. You will have covered your total base costs of doing business and the per hour variable costs of $375 (150 X $2.50 = $375) leaving a net profit of $125 for the month. As this example highlights, the more hours of services you provide, the higher the net profit will be. You must increase your hourly charges, work overtime (in excess of the 173 base hours), or hire help for whose service you can charge more than they cost you per hour, in order to increase your total earning profits.

The growing complexity of these numbers is best handled, when the company can afford it, by professional accountants. Your primary business will be providing services, whether by you or your employees. Seeking the assistance of professionals is generally a wise business decision.

ADVERTISING SERVICES

Unless you have a reliable source of client referrals, you will have to make some type of investment in advertising to maintain a client load sufficient to support yourself. If you are fortunate enough to have your peers referring their excess client load to you, or local gyms giving you referrals, you will not need advertising.

Advertising can be done in a variety of ways. It is simply locating your target market and making them aware of your services. This is another area where niche marketing will serve you well. With a small target market, you do not have to spend much money broadcasting your advertising to the general population. Focus your efforts in locations where your potential clientele will congregate. If you serve the obese, place flyers in the waiting lines at the local all-you-can-eat buffet. If you serve athletes, target the places where you find them working out.

With a little forethought, you can isolate locations frequented by your target clientele. In the example of targeting weight-loss services to those waiting in line at the full-service buffet, you are taking advantage of the fact that these folks are hungry and might be feeling a bit of remorse for their overeating. They are open to a subtle suggestion at this point. A flyer on the bulletin board with tear-off contact phone numbers can be effective.

Newspaper advertising is often effective, but is inefficient in that it is targeted broadly at the entire population. Classified ads are generally a good value and return valuable leads. Local trade publications sometimes offer free ads to increase circulation. As you go into local discount stores and other businesses, observe what free or low-cost publications are offered at the entry and exit doors. See what people are carrying and whether it has advertising available. If you target weight-loss clients, ask your local Overeaters Anonymous group if they accept any type of advertising for their membership.

Creativity is your friend when offering services to the public. Understand your potential clients, what they really desire (e.g., improving looks, healthier body, or longer life) and use these desires to attract their attention.

LOCATION – LOCATION – LOCATION

Consider carefully where you set up your business. If it is a large, established gym, you may have more access to clients, but you may also have more competition for those clients. You may not be able to make as much money because you may have to pay a gym owner a larger percentage of your fee, or there may be a cap on what you can charge.

A smaller gym may provide you with fewer clients, but might provide you the opportunity to charge more, and have less competition. You must decide what location is best. If you are an independent contractor, you might be able to work at more than one gym. This could add to your travel time, but it could provide you with more continuous revenue.

If you are considering opening up your own gym, you should have a real estate professional help you find the right location. It may be smart to look at your demographics again. In addition, you should consider whether you have the reputation to maintain your own place of business.

Look at where you are financially to decide if the location you are in is making you the most money. Include in your analysis what your competition is making at different locations. Consider your situation if you have an offer to move to another gym. You need to weigh the pros and cons. If you signed a no-competition agreement, you cannot take your clientele with you.

IRS FORMS AND ISSUES

Never underestimate the IRS. Their job has created a rather complicated web of forms, laws, and rules for even small business owners like you. If you have your accounts in order at tax time, the process will be much quicker and smoother. It is always better to do it correctly the first time. Do not wait until tax time to start thinking about taxes. If you have kept up with your financial records, when it comes time to fill out the forms, your job should be easy. The forms are mostly about plugging in numbers from your profit and loss statement and income and expense ledgers.

It is advisable to earmark a portion of your income and financial assets for taxes — 20 to 25 percent is a good start. Anything left over can be used as a capital investment fund or bonus. This is especially important for sole proprietors who have to pay self-employment tax, which makes up your share of Social Security and Medicare payments.

BUSINESS PERMITS AND LICENSES

Depending on where you live, you will need a business permit or license. If you do not have the proper permits, you could be conducting business illegally. Most areas require at minimum a county or city license. This is even true if you are conducting business out of your home. In addition to the local licensing, there may be county, state, or federal licensing requirements as well. The good news is the fees for these types of permits are usually low. You may run into problems with zoning issues if you are conducting a business in an area zoned for residential. Do not try to conduct business without these permits, or you could be fined or even arrested. You can get a zoning variance from the municipal planning commission in some cases, since your type of work will not increase the traffic in an area.

You might have another business, such as health shake mixes, that will require a permit from a health inspector. If you are planning on doing major renovating or remodeling at your house to make a home office, you may be required to get a building permit.

As a personal trainer, you will not need to get a federal license unless you decide to engage in some activity that is regulated by the government like the Food and Drug Administration.

To get your business permit, you should go to city hall or the county courthouse or call the clerk's office to find out where you need to get a permit, what you will need to bring, and what the fees will be.

WHAT IS A FEDERAL ID NUMBER? DO I NEED ONE?

In certain cases, the federal government may require a small business to have an Employment Identification Number (EIN). You will need one if you choose to have any kind of business other than a sole proprietorship. If you plan to work independently, you can use your social security number as your identification number for tax purposes. Otherwise, you must apply for an EIN from the IRS.

In the application for your EIN, the IRS requires you to declare a fiscal year start and end. Certain states also require in their certificate of incorporation that you declare when your fiscal year begins. Most companies make the calendar year the same as their fiscal year. The second most popular choice is July 1 to June 30.

If you decide to incorporate, you will have to file two returns. The first half of your year, you file an individual return as a sole proprietor using Schedule C and any other schedules that are indicated. After the second half of your year, you would file a corporate return. You have a couple of choices; you could file a Form 1120, or Form 1120S if you make a Subchapter S election. You would also file an individual return, because you would be an employee of your own corporation.

There are some variations of this. If you choose April 1 to October 1 as the beginning of your fiscal year, you will file the same two sets of returns. However, if you choose April 1, you file as a sole proprietor for the first quarter, which runs January 1 to March 31.

In this case, you will file corporate and individual returns for the last three quarters — April 1 to December 31.

If October 1 is the beginning of your fiscal year, you will file as a sole proprietor for the first three quarters, which would be January 1 to September 30. You will file corporate and individual returns for the last quarter, which would run October 1 to December 31.

There is a benefit to declaring a separate fiscal year. It allows you more freedom in your tax planning. The savings that you and your accountant can accomplish through this freedom of planning can be significant. You should speak to an accountant or tax professional to decide which fiscal year would benefit you the most. In addition, you will have less tax forms to file.

On the other hand, there are some significant disadvantages to choosing a separate fiscal year. You will have to decide what the best plan is for you. As a sole proprietor, you may just wish to stick with having your fiscal year follow your calendar year.

The laws change frequently, and if an agent is not current on tax laws, he or she may not be very helpful. You can find the information you need from a selection of IRS publications, some of which are free. The IRS wants you to do your taxes right because they want their money, so try to use what they have to offer, especially if it is free. Any forms or publications you get from their Web site will be the most up-to-date forms available.

Υ For information concerning starting a business and keeping records, Publication 583 is a good source of information. **www.irs.gov/pub/irs-pdf/p583.pdf**

- ⵣ For a good reference guide when figuring out what taxes you need to pay and when, consider reading Publication 334. **www.irs.gov/pub/irs-pdf/p334.pdf**

- ⵣ Publication 509 will help you find answers about tax calendars and when certain taxes are due. **www.irs.gov/pub/irs-pdf/p509.pdf**

As a small business, you may need to pay estimated taxes, and Publication 505 may help answer some of your questions. **www.irs.gov/pub/irs-pdf/p505.pdf**

SELF-EMPLOYMENT TAX

In addition to other taxes, as a sole proprietor, partnership, or as an LLC making more than $400, you have to pay self-employment (SE) tax, which you file on the form 1040 schedule SE.

TAX TIP

You should save aside money to pay your taxes — 20 to 25 percent is a good amount to start with. If you have anything left over at tax time, you can reinvest it as a capital investment fund or a bonus. You can build an account dedicated to paying taxes. If you do not touch this, you can save yourself from scrambling for money later. This money can also pay for your Social Security and Medicare payments. It is important that you save and plan ahead.

ACCOUNTING ISSUES

There are a number of accounting programs, such as Microsoft Accounting and QuickBooks, that you may want to invest in. They will help you keep up with your finances, especially when it comes to tax time. You can also use these programs and upload the information to an accountant. This can be very helpful to both of you. If you want to be low-tech, a simple written ledger is all that is necessary.

Either of these forms of accounting will only work if you are putting the required information into them. You have to set time aside every day, or at least every few days, to input your invoices, payments, and bills. If you are not diligent in entering this information, you can fall behind or miss something, which can cost you money.

Keep all your receipts and invoices in one place. Invest in a small filing cabinet with file folders. Do not keep receipts and papers all over your house. Keep a clean, organized office. You will thank yourself later. Running a business is not just about fitness training; you have to spend the time doing the business end as well.

If you have employees, make sure you have a solid understanding of employee taxes, as these can be the trickiest taxes to deal with. You may come to a point in your personal training business where you will want to hire more employees. From a secretary to a person to help you set up a venue, you need to be prepared to commit 30 percent of your payroll to taxes and paperwork. It will be your responsibility to withhold all of your full- or part-time employees' federal and state income tax, Social Security, and Medicare taxes from paychecks. At tax time, you will need to remit them with your overall tax bill. In addition, you will have to pay your company's portion of Social Security and Medicare benefit funds. You must consider that, if you are paying employee salaries up to $87,922, you can expect to be taxed 6.2 percent for Social Security and 1.45 percent for Medicare.

Social Security and Medicare taxes pay for benefits that workers and families receive under the Federal Insurance Contributions Act (FICA). Social Security tax pays for benefits under the old age, survivors, and disability insurance part of FICA. Medicare tax pays for benefits under the hospital insurance part of FICA. You have to pay the portion of your employees' taxes that matches what you have withheld from them. You should use Forms 941 to file the federal, social security, and Medicare taxes. See **www. irs.gov/pub/irs-pdf/f941.pdf.**

You will also be responsible for Federal Unemployment Tax Act (FUTA) taxes. You have to pay this separately from other taxes. Your employees do not pay into this tax; you are totally responsible for it. This is another thing to consider before hiring others to work as employees in your personal training business. You will need to file a form 940 to cover the FUTA taxes. See **www. irs.gov/pub/irs-pdf/f940.pdf.**

Make sure you deposit the taxes in a financial institution that is able to hold these type funds.

Here is the calendar of when payroll taxes are due:

- April 30 for wages paid January — March

- July 31 for April — June

- October 31 for July — September

- January 31 for October — December

If you owe more taxes then $500, your due date changes to the fifteenth day of the next month.

INDEPENDENT CONTRACTORS

There is another option you may want to consider instead of hiring employees, and that is hiring independent contractors. Hiring independent contractors can save you paperwork and expenses. As a personal trainer, you will be more likely to hire these types of workers as your business grows. Having a list of independent contractors is a good thing to develop. There is also the advantage of having them available when you need a break or want to go on vacation.

The definition of an independent contractor is a worker who is in business for him- or herself, and who pays his or her own taxes and insurance. Independent contractors use their own equipment or facilities. One of the benefits of hiring independent contractors is that they require little or no supervision, and they are typically paid per session or group of sessions.

There are things you must consider when determining whether a worker is an employee or an independent contractor. This assists you in avoiding the threat of tax fraud and liability charges. You must make sure that the above factors apply to them and that these points are clear to the workers. You should be sure that you are using an independent contractor and not treating them as an employee. If you make a mistake, you could be liable for employment taxes for that worker and, in addition, you may be fined a penalty.

One of the best ways to ensure that you do not make any errors in using independent contractors is to develop and use a written independent contractor's agreement. On the following page is a sample of an independent contractor's contract. You can also find a copy of it on the CD-ROM. Be sure that you include the contractor's full name, address, and Social Security number or EIN.

A bonus of using an independent contractor is that you do not have to withhold or pay any taxes on payment you make to them. They are responsible for their own taxes. A gauge that is generally used with an independent contractor is that the person for whom the services are performed has the right to control or direct only the result of the work and not what will be done and how it will be done or the method of accomplishing the result.

Independent contractors are generally not employees. However, whether such people are employees or independent contractors is determined on a case-by-case basis. Independent contractors are subject to self-employment tax. You will need to make sure that all of your independent contractors complete an FDIC Substitute Form W-9 Request for Taxpayer Identification Number and Certification. This form provides the independent contractor's correct taxpayer identification number to you. You will be required to file Form 1099-MISC, Miscellaneous Income, to report payments of $600 or more to persons who are independent contractors you may use in the course of doing business. See **www.irs.gov/pub/irs-pdf/fw9.pdf.**

INDEPENDENT CONTRACTOR AGREEMENT

This agreement is made on _____, 20 _____, between _____
_____, owner, of _____
_____, City of _____, State of _____,
and _____, contractor,
of _____
_____, City of _____, State of _____.

For valuable consideration, the owner and contractor agree as follows:

1. The independent contractor agrees to furnish all the labor and materials to do the following work for the owner as an independent contractor:

2. The contractor agrees that the following portions of the total work will be completed by the dates specified:

INDEPENDENT CONTRACTOR AGREEMENT

3. The contractor agrees to perform this work in a professional manner according to standard practices. If any plans or specifications are part of this job, they are attached to and are part of this agreement.

4. The owner agrees to pay the contractor as full payment $_____, for doing the work outlined above. This price will be paid to the contractor upon satisfactory completion of the work in the following manner and on the following dates: _____

   _____

5. The contractor and the owner may agree to extra services and work, but any such extras must be set out and agreed to in writing by both the contractor and the owner.

6. The contractor agrees to indemnify and hold the owner harmless from any claims or liability arising from the contractor's work under this agreement.

7. No modification of this agreement will be effective unless it is in writing and is signed by both parties. This agreement binds and benefits both parties and any successors. This document, including any attachments, is the entire agreement between the parties. This agreement is governed by the laws of the State of ____.

Dated:_____, 20 _____

_____
Signature of Owner

_____
Printed Name of Owner

_____
Signature of Contractor

_____
Printed Name of Contractor

_____
Address

_____
EIN or Social Security Number

CONFIDENTIALITY ISSUES

You will often have to handle confidential files or information. Some clients may ask you to sign a confidentiality agreement. It is always advisable to have an attorney look over anything before you sign it.

You should take every precaution to protect your client's privacy. This is just good business practice. That means that you should not be gossiping about what you saw or heard during a session with your client. Your credibility can be severely damaged by gossip.

You should be careful not to send credit card information, Social Security numbers, dates of birth, or any other personal information over the Internet; it is too vulnerable to theft and use. If you have any of this information in your files and need to purge those records, make sure that they are shredded. There are a number of good shredders that can be bought at office supply stores. All you receipts, contracts, bills, and anything else that has identifying information should be shredded, not just thrown away. Thieves will go through dumpsters to find personal information to use illegally.

DESKTOP PROGRAMS THAT CAN HELP

Here are a few programs that can help you keep up with your finances:

- Y **Quicken** — This program comes in a few different versions and basically acts like an electronic checkbook. You can download your balances from online and use the information to help you at tax time, as the information can be downloaded to some tax software. If you have kept good records and put items in appropriate categories, finding deductions will be easier.

Y **Tax Cut** — This program is created by H&R Block. It asks you questions and you fill in the data based upon your records. They also offer state versions that download the information you input for your federal return. You can file your taxes electronically for a fee.

Y **TurboTax** — This is another popular program that offers many of the same features that Tax Cut does. Both programs cost about $40. If you are comfortable doing your own taxes, either of these programs will be helpful.

IS YOUR PERSONAL TRAINING A BUSINESS OR A HOBBY?

You should decide early on whether your personal training is a hobby or a business. It will make a difference when it comes to your taxes. The difference between a job and a hobby is that you do not expect to make a profit from a hobby. If you decide you will not make a profit at personal training, there is a limit on the deductions you can take.

On your tax returns, you must include any income you make from your hobby. If you just like performing your personal training services for friends and family for a small fee, you must include this on your tax returns. If you make a significant profit from it, you should not consider it a hobby. On your taxes, you cannot use a loss from personal training activities to offset other income. Personal training activities you do as a hobby come under this limit.

The limit on not-for-profit losses applies to individuals, partnerships, estates, trusts, and S corporations. However, this limit does not apply to corporations other than S corporations.

To help you determine if your personal training business is an activity for profit, you should consider the following:

- Y Do you conduct your personal training activities in a businesslike manner?

- Y Does the time and effort you put into personal training indicate that you intend to make it a profitable venture?

- Y Do you depend on income you make from personal training as your main source of income and rely on it as your livelihood?

- Y Are your losses due to circumstances beyond your control or are they normal in the startup phase of your type of business?

- Y Have you changed your methods of doing business in an attempt to improve your profitability?

- Y Do you and those who are supporting you have the experience, knowledge, and skills to create a successful business?

- Y Have you made a profit doing similar activities in the past? What is that profit?

- Y Does your personal training make some profit some years?

Y Do you expect to make a future profit from the appreciation of the assets used in your personal training activities?

DEPRECIATION

Another thing you need to consider when doing your taxes is depreciation. The equipment that you use often ages or becomes obsolete. It is important that you keep clear records of what you buy. If you are using equipment that you bought before you started your personal training business, you may depreciate the equipment based on their market value at the time you began using it for business. Any major repairs and improvements may also be depreciated. The other requirement for being able to depreciate equipment is that it must be used in your personal training business. This may seem obvious, but you cannot use your television in your living room as an asset just because you watched a bodybuilding competition on it. You must use the equipment mostly for business purposes. Cell phones are one item you must consider. You are better off using a dedicated phone for your business so that there is not any question of whether it can be used as a business asset.

Depreciation ends when you have recovered its cost or retired it from service. The kind of property you own affects how you can claim a depreciation deduction. There are two types of property you will have in your business: tangible and intangible.

Tangible property is real property that can be seen or touched. There are two types of tangible property: real property, which is immovable property; and personal property, which is moveable property. Examples of real property are buildings and land. Examples of personal property are cars, machinery, or equipment.

Certain types of property cannot be depreciated. An example of this is land, because it cannot wear out or become obsolete.

In contrast, intangible property is property that cannot be seen or touched. Examples of this type of asset are copyrights, franchises, or patents. Some of these assets cannot be depreciated, and must be amortized instead. If you have questions of whether you should depreciate or amortize, you should use Form 4562, Depreciation and Amortization. See **www.irs.gov/pub/irs-pdf/f4562.pdf.**

You do have the option of deducting all or part of the cost of certain qualifying property used in your business in the year you placed it in service. You can do this by claiming a Section 179 deduction. The bonus of claiming the Section 179 deduction is that you get to deduct more value of the asset in the beginning. The rule is that you must claim the Section 179 deduction only when your property is ready to be used in your personal training business. In 2007, the cost of qualifying property was $125,000. This limit is reduced by the amount by which the cost of qualified property placed in service during the tax year exceeds $500,000. Another rule is that you cannot deduct costs in excess of your taxable income. If you decide to use the section 179 deduction, you will need to use form 4562.

You may also decide that your tax burden will be minimal due to your business not doing very well. In this case, you may decide not to claim this deduction. In this case, you can choose to write the costs according to depreciation of any or all items with a life of over one year. You will deduct the cost of an item divided over a period of years. The length of this type of depreciation can range from three to thirty nine years, depending on the type of property you are considering. The larger the amount, the, longer the depreciation.

AVOIDING AN AUDIT

The simplest way to avoid an audit is to keep good records. Your return must have supporting documentation of any income, expenses, and credits you report. If you kept good records to begin with, this should not be a problem. If the IRS decides to audit your tax returns, the auditor may ask you to explain the items reported. Having all your receipts accounted for with complete records can make this a painless, quick process. You should have either electronic or paper accounting journals and ledgers. In these business books, you must show your gross income, as well as your deductions and credits. Some of the items you should have available are any sales slips, paid bills, invoices, receipts, deposit slips, and canceled checks. After you have filed a return, you should store these records along with a copy of your return in a safe place. In a shoebox in your closet may not be ideal, but knowing where the records are and that they are organized is what is important. A rule of thumb is to keep your taxes and records for at least four years. It is up to you to prove entries, deductions, and statements you made on your tax returns. If you have good records, this "burden of proof" should not be a problem.

When the four years has elapsed on a particular set of financial records, do not discard them until you check to see whether you have to keep them longer for other purposes.

WHEN TO HIRE AN ACCOUNTANT

If you can afford it, you should try to hire an accountant from day one, especially if you are not good with numbers. You need to be honest with yourself concerning this, because if you do your taxes wrong, you could lose not only your job, but your personal assets as well — especially if you are a sole proprietor. Try to get an accountant who is familiar with personal training. This can be a great benefit because they can have a working understanding of your business and what kinds of taxes you will owe, as well as specific deductions you can take. If the accountant is familiar with working with a business of your size, he or she can help keep you on track as far as deadlines. An accountant can help you set up any financial software from the beginning, and can set the books up in a way that can better help you run your business.

Tip

Make sure that you eat after you train. Your body needs nutrients for energy. A sports drink is only temporary fuel. It is best to eat complex carbs and protein within 90 minutes of your workout.

Making Your Business as Solid as Your Body

7

Just as your body needs food and water to keep it strong and healthy, your personal training business will need certain things to keep it operating at an optimal level. Some of these include maintaining proper records, setting cancellation policies, paying taxes, and more. Initiating these practices early on in your business will help your business run more smoothly.

LEGAL FORMS

To protect you and your business from liability due to litigious individuals, seek the counsel of a good attorney who can assist you with creating legal forms that will help you to operate your personal training business without fear of being sued. Having these legal forms available for your clients to sign prior to training them could mean all the difference in your bottom line if you were to be sued.

Accident Report Form

Suppose your client pulls a muscle while stretching, how will you document this injury? You will need an Accident Report Form. The purpose of this form is to document your clients' injuries while they are in your care. On this form, you will need to document the date, location, time, and nature of the injury; if there were any witnesses; and what exercises were being performed when your client was injured. You may want to include how the injury was treated and any follow up that was performed after the injury. It is imperative to obtain the injured client's signature on the form as soon as it is reasonably possible. Also, obtain signatures of any witnesses to the injury.

It may seem tedious to fill out these forms, but doing so may protect your financial interests in the event that your client wants to pursue litigation. Most states require that you maintain the Accident Report Form for seven years.

Waiver Form

The Waiver Form states that your client will not hold your companies liable for damages if they were to say, have a stroke during aerobics. In addition, the Waiver Form states that the client has disclosed all medical conditions prior to training. Having your clients sign a Waiver Form will prevent them from blaming you for their injuries while in your care.

Disclaimer and Informed Consent Form

Clients will sign this form to confirm that they are aware of the fact that injuries may occur as a result of personal training and that they have disclosed to you any mental or physical ailments that may preclude them from successfully training with you.

Having your client complete this form prior to training serves two purposes: First, you will be able to tailor a program around your client's strengths and weaknesses. Second, you will be released of any liability if your client is injured because of any preexisting mental or physical conditions while training with you.

INSURANCE

Starting out in your new business, it may be your first instinct to cut out certain expenditures that seem unnecessary, such as an extra telephone line, a Web site, or advertisements. However, one worthwhile expense is insurance. Insurance is necessary if you are training anyone other than yourself because carrying insurance limits your liability if you were to find yourself named as the main party in a lawsuit. Having insurance will protect you, your business, your employees, and your assets.

There are several types of insurance, and each serves a different purpose. Enlisting the services of an attorney may help to clarify which insurance will best protect your financial interests. Most of the personal trainers I have consulted with at the end of this book say that they carry liability insurance. It can be costly to go through a lawsuit. If you are a sole proprietor, you could risk losing your house, car, and other assets. That is why it only makes sense to have liability insurance. Being an LLC does not totally protect you from being sued. There are situations in which you can be sued for negligence or bad business practices.

Personal liability insurance will protect you and even your gym and equipment. It will be hard to continue to do business if all of your expensive equipment is liquidated. There are different types of liability insurance that you should consider depending, on your situation.

Types of Business Liability Insurance

General Liability Insurance: You should consider buying this form of business liability insurance as a personal trainer. This type of insurance will protect your business from lawsuits and liability. Included is protection in suits involving injury claims, property damages, and advertising claims. For most personal trainers, general liability insurance, also known as commercial general liability (CGL), is the only type of insurance they may need to buy.

Professional Liability Insurance: If you are providing other services in addition to personal training, such as nutrition counseling, you will need this type of insurance. This type of liability insurance is known as "errors and omissions." This coverage protects your business against malpractice, errors, negligence, and omissions. It may be a legal requirement, and some personal trainers may be required by a gym or other facility to carry this type of insurance.

Product Liability Insurance: If you are offering products that you are selling or manufacturing, you should be protected in the event a person becomes injured using the product. If you are selling herbal supplements or products, such as whey protein, you should carry this type of liability insurance. Imagine if you sold a protein shake that had nuts to someone who was allergic to them. The amount of coverage and the level of risk depend on your business type. The level of risk your products pose will determine the cost of this type of coverage.

Shopping for Insurance

Personal trainers renewing an existing policy or starting a new policy need to shop for the best business liability insurance rates and coverage. Here are some tips that can help you get the best prices.

Belong to an Association: There are many trade associations and business groups, such as your local chamber of commerce, that provide members the benefit of purchasing insurance at group rates. Some associations specialize in personal trainer insurance. Here are links to some of the places where you can find this type of specialized insurance. Other companies that offer liability insurance can be found in fitness and training trade magazines.

Idea Health and Fitness Association
w2.ideafit.com/membership/personal-trainer-insurance

Sadler Sports and Recreation Insurance
www.sadlersports.com/personaltrainerinsurance

Markel Insurance Company
www.markelfitness.com/Personal+Trainers

NESTA National Exercise and Sports Trainers Association
www.nestacertified.com

National Strength and Conditioning Association
www.nsca-lift.org/Membership/WhyJoin/Benefits/insurance.shtml

National Federation of Professional Trainers
www.nfpt.com/resources.htm

Compare coverage: The extent of business liability coverage varies from insurer to insurer. You need to do your research and consider if and how much legal fees are covered. Review the policy details to know what is included and excluded in the coverage. Do not sign anything until you are sure that you are fully covered.

To gain a better perspective of the amount of coverage your personal training business needs, look at the health and fitness industry. Review the recent legal actions and settlements in the personal trainer field. Talk to peers and find their level of coverage. Using your peer feedback and personal trainer industry research, determine the average legal costs and settlement to set your coverage limits.

Get the package deal: Purchasing separate types of business insurance from various insurers can quickly increase your premiums. You need to take a close look at your business needs. You may determine that it makes sense to buy a package of policies such as a business owner's policy (BOP) to cover your business and save on rates. Be sure to understand the extent of coverage of the package. Not every type of insurance falls under a BOP.

Find a specialist broker: Your personal trainer business and the fitness industry has unique needs and risks. To get the best available coverage and rates, consider working with an insurance broker who knows your business and has experience in your industry.

Protecting your personal trainer business from risks is the foundation for success. Take the necessary time to investigate your business liability insurance needs with an insurance representative, your industry association, and peers. It could be the most important decision to your business's survival.

Medical Insurance

You are in the business of personal training, thus, you should have medical insurance in the event that you are ill or injured. Medical insurance can range in cost and coverage.

If you are employed at a health club, check with your employer to see if they offer a plan that meets your needs. If you are self-employed, you will need to contact an insurance company that specializes in health coverage for you and your employees. Offering insurance for your employees is a good benefit and aids in employee satisfaction when your employees knows that they can work without worrying about how they will pay for their medical bills.

Some resources that may assist you in your medical insurance search include:

   Y www.ihrsa.org/buyersmart

   Y www.trainerinsurance.com

   Y www.sportsfintness.com

   Y www.kandkinsurance.com

Disability Insurance

This type of insurance provides coverage for you in the event that you are disabled long-term. As an employee for a health club, you may already have this insurance; however, most employers do not provide coverage. If you are self-employed, you will have to purchase coverage for you and your employees. Personal training is an injurious profession, thus having disability coverage makes long-term financial sense.

Business Owner's Policies

BOPs are plans that offer several types of insurance in one package. The plan may include policies for business interruption and for property insurance. This type of insurance is for personal trainers who own or lease the property for which they train their clients. This usually does not cover professional liability coverage.

Worker's Compensation

If you have ever been injured on your job, chances are you have heard of Worker's Compensation. If you decide to hire employees, the law mandates that you provide coverage for your employees. Rates depend on the number of employees you have, the type of jobs that they perform, and your history of claims. If you decide not to carry Worker's Compensation or carry an insufficient coverage amount, you will be subject to state and federal government fines.

Running your personal training operation requires some investment in insurance at some point. When choosing coverage and types, consider the following:

- Do you have employees?

- Are you certified?

- Do you own your location?

Y Has your location moved?

Y Did you buy new equipment?

It is a good idea to assess your needs by answering the above questions on an annual basis, so that you will always have the correct amount of coverage. Once you select the proper coverage, it is a good idea to keep receipts for all payments and deductibles for your records.

MAINTAINING RECORDS

It is worth the expense to buy good bookkeeping software. Make sure you have a good backup and try to keep hard copies. Make sure that your software is updatable, that it can let you know when and what taxes you need to pay, and that you have a reminder that will let you know when to do certain bookkeeping functions.

As for business expenses, you cannot call every meal and vacation a business expense. For an item to qualify as a deduction, expenses must be business-related, ordinary, necessary, and reasonable. The best way to keep a close eye on your business expenses is to pay for items from your business account. When you do this, you should make sure to enter your qualifying expenses in the appropriate expense ledger category and keep all receipts.

The correct way to record your expenses is to record what you actually paid out. Do not use the market value. You cannot deduct interest charges on your purchases. If you engage in any type of barter economy, you should know that it is treated like any other business income based on fair market value.

You may have questions about startup costs. Deducting these expenses can be more complicated, and you may want to rely on the advice and assistance of an accountant or tax professional. If you choose to tackle business-related startup expenses on your own, here is what you need to know. Startup expenses can be deducted two different ways. The first is that it may be capitalized at the time you quit or sell your business. The second is that these costs can be amortized monthly over a 60-month period.

Business deductions can only be deducted if the activity was undertaken with the intent of making a profit. That means if you meet with one of your friends for lunch and they are a caterer, the lunch has to be about making a partnership or to discuss a business merger. It cannot be about talking about old times and how business is going for both of you. It has to be for the express purpose of making a profit. It is a good idea to write down on the receipt what the purpose of the expense was and make sure you write it in your ledger as well. The longer you wait, the harder it will be to remember.

You cannot necessarily make deductions the first year you are in business. The IRS often states that you have to be making a profit and be a viable business before you can begin making deductions. You can meet this requirement by making a profit in any two years of a five-year period. When you reach this requirement, you can begin deducting business expenses such as supplies, subscriptions to professional journals, and an allowance for the business use of your car or truck.

If you are working from home, you can make deductions such as utilities, and in some cases, even a new paint job on your home, if this helps improve your business. Remember that the IRS is going to treat the part of your home you use for business as if it is a business and not part of the rest of the home. You have to be diligent in making sure you have clear, concise records, and make sure that you do not to mix business and personal matters.

In addition to helping you out at tax time, good record keeping can help you to monitor the progress of your business. Good records can show you whether your personal training business is growing or failing. It can show you where you need to make improvements and can signal you to make a new market analysis. If you are not attracting the right clients, your figures will show it. The better your records are, the greater chance your personal training business has in succeeding.

All of your financial records should be as accurate as possible. This can help you prevent an audit. In addition, these records can help you when you need to deal with your bank and creditors. Your records should include income, or profit and loss, statements and balance sheets. An income statement will show the income and expenses of your personal training business over a period of time. In your balance sheet, it will show your assets, liabilities, and equity on any given date. As a personal trainer, you will receive money from many sources and clients. You need to be sure that your records can identify the source of your receipts. That is why writing down who gave you the money, what for, and on what date is important. This is the same procedure for any business-related expenses.

Some of the supporting documentation that you may want to keep for your records includes sales records, cash receipts, accounts receivable, and accounts payable. In addition, three financial statements that you as a business owner may want to use in your personal training business on a regular basis are the Profit and Loss Statement, Balance Sheet, and Cash Flow Statement.

The Profit and Loss Statement, also known as the P&L Statement or the Income Statement, is a snapshot of the financial health of your business at any given moment in time, such as monthly, quarterly, or annually.

A Balance Sheet is a table that illustrates the assets, liabilities, and capital of your business either monthly, quarterly, or annually. It is normally generated when the accounting period is closed.

The Cash Flow Statement focuses on the flow of cash in and out of your business and, just like the other financial statements, it can be generated monthly, quarterly, or annually.

After you have accumulated all of these financial documents, you will need to find a systematic manner in which to organize them. You can organize your records manually or by using software. If you choose to organize your records manually, keep all of your records in a file cabinet. Using an accounting ledger, which can be purchased at a stationery store or office supply store, will benefit you, because you can record all of your income and expenses in it.

On the other hand, if "keeping the books" manually proves to be time consuming, you may elect to use financial software programs, such as Quicken. With these programs, you can print financial reports, graphs, and charts.

Yet another alternative may be to hire a company that specializes in financial record keeping. These companies may allow you to utilize their software free of charge, but may charge a monthly fee for additional services, such as Electronic Funds Transfer, credit card processing, billing, and collections.

No matter how you decide to keep your financial records, the key point to remember is to be consistent and organized. Below are some resources that may assist you in maintaining good financial records:

Software Companies

- ABC Financial — **www.abcfinancial.com**

- ASF International — **www.asfint.com**

- CSI Software — **www.csisoftwareusa.com**

- efit Financial — **www.efitfinancial.com**

- Twin Oaks — **www.tosd.com**

Books

Entrepreneurship for Dummies by Kathleen Allen (Wiley).

Financial Statements: A Step-By-Step Guide to Understanding and Creating Financial Reports by Thomas R. Ittelson (Career Press).

Managing by the Numbers: A Commonsense Guide to Understanding and Using Your Company's Financials: An Essential Resource for Growing Businesses by Chuck Kremer (Perseus Book Group).

Client Records

Just like maintaining good financial records helps you keep your finger on the pulse of the financial health of your personal training business, maintaining good client files will help you to keep track of the progress of your clients' health.

Some records that you may want to keep in a client file include:

- Activity Log

- Exercise Prescription Form

- Exercise Results Form

- Fitness Assessment Form

- Goal Sheet

- Informed Consent Form

- Initial Consultation Form

- Medical History Form

- Membership Application

- Prospect Lead Sheet

- Session Log

- Workout Log

To obtain sample forms that are used in client files, please visit **www.wiley.com/go/personaltrainer.**

Personnel Records

If you are able to add staff to your personnel training business, you will need to maintain personnel files for each employee. Some of the records that you may want to keep in your employees' personnel files are: the W-4, which is used for tax withholding; the I-9, which is used to confirm whether the employee is legally able to work in the United States; the job application; and any results from drug, background, or placement tests given prior to the employee being hired. Maintaining these records will keep you in compliance with federal and labor laws.

HIRING AND FIRING

So, you have decided that you need to hire additional help for your personal training business. You may be wondering whom to hire, where to find employees, and what the costs are. Following is information that will help:

Whom Do I Hire?

Choosing an employee depends on your financial situation. You can either hire a trainer as an employee or as an independent contractor. There are some points to consider for both. If you hire a trainer to be your employee, you will have to pay Worker's Compensation, Social Security and Medicare Tax, and Federal Unemployment Tax.

On the other hand, if you hire a trainer as an independent contractor, you will only need to pay the trainer's salary and file a Form 1099 with the IRS at the end of the year.

Where Do I Find Employees?

You have several options for locating potential employees. One option is to place a help-wanted advertisement in your local newspaper. Another option is by word of mouth. Yet another option is to contact the organization by which you were certified to inquire about placing an ad on their Web site or in their newsletters. These are just some ideas to get you started.

How Much Will It Cost?

Hiring an employee will cost more than just paying a salary; you will have to pay Worker's Compensation insurance and Unemployment Insurance, and you will have to match the Social Security and Medicare taxes, also known as FICA, for your employee. All of the above is in addition to the salary that you will have to pay.

If the costs of hiring an employee are too steep, then hiring an independent contractor may prove to be more cost effective. One point to remember is to submit the Form 1099 for the contractor at year's end.

Now that you have found candidates for the job that you are trying to fill, assessments, interviews, and observation are good ways to find out how suitable the potential candidate may be. Assessments can range from written to practical and may include completing a test with questions from a certification test or giving the candidate hypothetical scenarios, such as asking questions like, "What would you do if your client injured themselves while bench pressing?"

Interviewing the candidate can yield important information, depending on the type of questions asked. Lastly, observing the potential trainer interacting with other staff and clients prior to being hired could also prove useful.

Unfortunately, there may come a time where the employer-employee relationship with one of your trainers may no longer be a viable one. In this case, you may have to fire them. Although this process may seem intimidating, following are some suggestions that will help to minimize your legal ramifications:

- Familiarize yourself with the basic labor laws

- Consult with an attorney

- Maintain detailed records of disciplinary actions and employee violations

PAYMENT AND COLLECTIONS

Although you may be in the business of helping your clients obtain their physical fitness dreams, at some point, you will want to be paid for your efforts. You need to determine how your clients will pay you, how you will collect their payments, what will happen if a client bounces a check, how you will charge a client who cancels a session, and how you will you handle your taxes. In this section, you will gain some insight on how to handle these financial questions with ease. Setting up payment and collection practices early on in your business can make or break you financially later on.

Payment Policies

Every business has payment policies. What type of payment policies your business will have depends on your personal preferences. You will need to balance your cash flow needs with the payment preferences of your clients. There are three main ways that a client can pay for their sessions with you: advance payments, end of session payments, or billed payments. Consider the pros and cons of each method.

Getting a lump sum payment for three months of sessions would be appealing to most personal trainers. The pros are that you will have your payments up front and your clients will be locked into their sessions. If your client misses a session, you do not have to worry since it is already paid. The cons are that if you have not perfected the art of money management, your client's advanced payments can be spent before you are set to re-bill your client. In addition, your client may request a discounted rate since they are prepaying.

Many states require personal trainers to be bonded before they are able to accept advanced payments from clients. This is to discourage dishonest trainers from collecting large sums of money from their clients and then disappearing before the client has had an opportunity to have their session.

You could elect to charge your client at the end of his or her session. This may be beneficial to you, because you will always have a steady stream of income coming in from your clients. In addition, you may elect to bill your clients for their services. This would be accomplished utilizing the infamous invoice. An invoice can be sent monthly, and it may include information such as the business name, invoice due date, amount due, and payment address.

Collection Procedures

You now know how your clients will pay you, but you have to know what method of payment they will use. If you are a one-person operation, you may want to accept only cash from your clients. On the other hand, if you want the ability to allow your clients to purchase more sessions, consider offering your clients the option of paying via credit card. Each payment method will have its benefits and disadvantages. Consider these when selecting your payment method choice. The four main methods that you may consider offering your clients are cash, check, electronics fund transfer (EFT), and credit card.

Checks and EFT are similar, because funds are deducted from the client's bank account. These methods are convenient for you, the business owner, because there is no fee unless the client has insufficient funds. Both of these methods leave a paper trail for both you and the client.

On the other hand, accepting cash from your client may be convenient if you do not want the hassle of wondering if a client's check will bounce. One point to remember with cash is that you may need to obtain a safe at your business location until you are able to make your regular bank deposits

Accepting credit cards is beneficial because clients will normally purchase larger blocks of sessions. The downside for you as the trainer may be that you might have to pay a transaction or processing fee, depending on which credit card you accept.

Billing

You know how your clients will pay and which method of payment they will use, now you will need to figure out how to bill them.

Billing can be done with house accounts, accounts on file, or invoices. Which one you decide to use depends on your situation.

A house account, which is similar to a bar tab, allows the client to get sessions for a specified period and then make payment thereafter. Some points to consider when setting up this form of billing are that you may want to create and give your client a signed copy of the house account terms and rules so they know what to expect. In addition, you may want to allocate a limit on the amount of sessions that a client can be billed before they have to pay. Yet another option for billing your clients is to maintain a copy of their credit card on file. For this option, you will need to be very cautious in protecting your client's financial information.

CANCELLATION

During your personal training business career, you will inevitably encounter clients who cancel their appointment at the last minute, or do not show up at all. You will need to address these situations with what is called a cancellation policy.

A cancellation policy is protection for your time and money. If a client does not show up for his or her appointment, you will at least have an opportunity to recoup the lost earnings by scheduling another client during that time slot.

A good cancellation policy will be in written form that the client can sign. It should address the consequences for each cancellation incidence. The policy should also address the time frame for which a client can reschedule before they will be charged a cancellation fee. For example, you may offer your client an opportunity to cancel their session within 24 hours before they are charged.

No-show sessions should also be addressed. Some personal trainers allow their clients one incidence of a no-show and any further occurrences will be billed a full session price.

How you decide to create your cancellation policy is up to you. The important thing to remember is to be fair and flexible. Be sure to have your client acknowledge the cancellation policy by going over the policy with them and having them sign a copy. This will ensure that the client understands what is expected before they train.

Tip

Get enough sleep at night. Most people need between 7 and 8 hours for their body to recooperate. It is also best to make sure that you have a regular sleep pattern for best workout results.

Working With Clients

8

CONSULTATIONS THAT LOCK IN CLIENTS

Many personal trainers offer free consultations. The purpose of these meetings is to ascertain whether you and the client will be a good fit for one another. In addition, the initial consultation allows you an opportunity to gather information about your potential clients' health before working with them. During the consultation, you will have to provide the client with many forms and ask probing questions. Hopefully, by the end of the consultation, you will have landed a client and will have scheduled his or her first session.

Planning the Consultation — What Will It Include?

The initial consultation will be your opportunity to learn in-depth information about your potential client. You will be reviewing a variety of forms, reviewing medical and exercise history, and identifying fitness goals with them. In addition, you will have an opportunity to present options to the client that will demonstrate how you, as a personal trainer, can meet their fitness goals.

Forms You Should Bring to the Initial Consultation

1. Initial Consultation Sheet

2. Medical History Form

3. Typical Day Sheet

4. Exercise History Sheet

5. Packages and Pricing Sheet

6. Client Agreement Form

7. Waiver of Liability

8. Cancellation Policy

9. Refund Policy

10. First Session Expectation Sheet

MEDICAL REVIEW

It is prudent to ascertain medical information about your prospective client prior to creating their exercise regimen. Key information that you will want to discover includes prior surgeries and current ailments they may be experiencing. In addition, you will want to learn of any medications they currently may be taking.

Appendix A:
Case Studies

Bryan J Pettit – BS, CSCS

GoldenTrainer Performance Studio Inc.

1066 Center Point RD NE

Cedar Rapids, Iowa 52402

www.goldentrainer.com

In 2002, I graduated from Iowa State University with my degree in Exercise and Sport Science, and started to work in Coralville, Iowa. In 2002, I took my initial training test through International Sports and Science Association (ISSA) and passed successfully. I decided I would take my knowledge to Cedar Rapids (where I was born and raised) where I became a fitness professional. I opened GoldenTrainer.com on March 4, 2003, as a means of communication for friends, family, and clients who moved to other parts of the country and world. In 2004, I completed the curriculum and passed my test through ISSA to become a specialist in Performance Nutrition. I take pride in serving people as individuals and not numbers, and in return, I receive a lot of praise and have many patrons who know they can e-mail, call, or stop in anytime and get their questions answered. Other companies will turn the phones off if it is not nine-to-five, and will not respond within one hour, let alone 24 hours, to e-mails.

CASE STUDY: BRYAN J. PETTIT

On January 15, 2005, I became the first person in Cedar Rapids, Iowa, to open a private one-on-one training studio when I opened Golden Trainer Performance Studio Inc. I had heard several complaints from my clients about having to deal with people in the gym who were sitting and talking on equipment, gawking at them while they trained, or just having to deal with those who were not taking the gym atmosphere seriously. I opened the business as a C-corporation (as advised by my attorney) to separate business and personal liability because of the amount of risk of injury. Now I have a much more serious clientele made up of everyday people, athletes, bodybuilders, and stay-at-home moms. Those who are not there for serious reasons, do not stick around long. Those who want to see results, I continue phone, e-mail, and other forms of contact after their training ends.

In 2007, I passed the test to become a Certified Strength & Conditioning Specialist (CSCS) through the National Strength & Conditioning Association (NSCA) to set myself further apart from the rest because of their requirement of a legitimate four-year degree and transcript to even take their test. I continue to spend much of the year taking continuing education tests, and attending seminars and classes both in and out of my Golden Trainer Performance Studio to be sure I am able to pass on up-to-date information to all of my clients.

If you have questions, or are looking for recommendations in your hometown for fitness professionals, I have become acquainted with others in our profession

CASE STUDY: BRYAN J. PETTIT

around the world and would love to recommend others to you. If you are a fitness professional or facility owner, we offer extra discounts and wholesale all products in bulk. We are always looking to network with others and feel that when competition comes together, it only makes us better. The benefits are the satisfaction of working with people and helping them improve their health and life style. The downside that many people do not think about before entering the field is the hours. Most people work roughly the same hours of 8 a.m. to 5 p.m. or 9 a.m. to 6 p.m. This creates early mornings and late evenings for someone entering the field to build a clientele. I would recommend personal training in Iowa to someone who is not afraid to work. The amount that one will charge in fees will be determined by one's overhead cost to run a facility and attend continuing education seminars. If someone feels that education is not a necessity and are unwilling to put the time in to stay up-to-date with their education in training and CPR (as I have), or if they are unwilling to put in the time needed to get the bills paid, they are not allowing themselves the opportunity to be successful.

SEABRON SKIP PAGE JR.

Seabron Skip Page Jr.

Challenge Group Health & Fitness, Inc.

8310 Cheyenne

Detroit, MI 48228

313-846-6700 Business Line

313-557-0762 Fax Line

313-646-7603 Cellular

SEABRON SKIP PAGE JR.

Seabron Skip Page, personal trainer and distributor of health products, describes himself as a coach to aid any individual in this life that crosses my path. The basics of training are core, strength, and power, and the emphasis of the meaning of these attributes of training are explained in absolute detail when consulting with a client.

I began practicing as a personal trainer in the year 1980. I was bored on a job that just was not enough for me, and I needed a stimulant for my life that meant something. Progressing out of my youth as a 30-year-old, satisfying that athletic urge, I supposed I had missed my life's calling. I needed a new challenge or a career change. My original business began in 1995, as a sole proprietorship, and I was certified by the IFPA. (International Fitness Professionals Association) in 1996.

Certification is a good item to include in your educational repertoire. Certification helps with the branding of your business, but passion, experience, and knowledge mean more to your respectability than the actual certification. Certification helps with the understanding of the national protocol; in other words to be abreast of what everyone else is doing in their practice of the business of personal fitness training. For example, the National Academy of Sports Medicine, (NASM) the latest certification organization on the block, brought about the newer technology of core development as well as other research that increased training knowledge, and trainers are becoming certified under that current training body of knowledge. To me, the serious practice of the life style is a greater resource for your knowledge base than any certification. Certification is really icing on the cake, which increases your base for understanding the industry.

I have bachelor's in E-business. I became fascinated by the Pentium computer in 1995 and discovered what it means to market a business online. If you decide to become a person who is interested in aiding others to improve their health, and you want to help guide people in your community on the ideals of practicing good health maintenance, you need as much education as you can get. I read *The Education of a Bodybuilder* by Arnold Schwarzenegger three times. Arnold said that when a person begins to seriously train, the first thing they want is a college degree, then they want to become a millionaire. When that happens, there is not enough time in the day to get done all that needs to be accomplished. This is what I call the representative

SEABRON SKIP PAGE JR.

of fitness training being the technology, or catalyst, for the uplifting of consciousness, due to the discipline of the 12-week training cycle. Minimally, there are community colleges that offer programs for two-year degrees that can give you a jump-start in tackling one of the major certifications on the market today. Certification organizations can help with marketing and sales, because you become part of a network, or individuals seeking personal training services, and you can call the organization like American College of Sports Medicine who will refer a trainer to you in the area where you live.

Initially, I began training and training others when I was 30 years old. I needed to lose excess weight brought on by drinking beer and eating peanut butter and jelly sandwiches, a habit I picked up in my earlier twenties. Every stage of life is a learning experience that teaches you something that ends in tragedy. Isn't that how we grow, by correcting the ills of the bad habits learned, and then correct those faults, turning them into meaningful learning experiences? I began to read every magazine, book, and manual — that began to establish my knowledge base, which for whatever reason, worked for me. As I studied these books and manuals, I trained and got my body into a condition that gave me a great deal of self-satisfaction. It actually took me out of a depression that I had not even realized had been plaguing for me much of my young life.

Establishing a network of organizations and individuals of like minds, and going to seminars is how you keep abreast of the industry, and the latest cycle of research which develops every so many years. I have attended seminars put on every year by the NSCA. My first was in Philadelphia in 1992, and the very next year, I attended the one in Las Vegas, which was a real thrill for me. I got seriously into program development, and I bought my first body composition machine put out by Futrex, the Futrex 5000A, and took it back to my marketplace in Detroit, where I lived, to put it through the rigors of test marketing. I was really not sure, at that time, if I even knew how to do that, but that was my challenge. I grew up with that machine, because it added to a new body of knowledge that I craved to learn about. It was a very expensive endeavor because I purchased that equipment for about $3000 on a 12-month lease.

Consultation with a new or inquiring client is a beginning body of work, aiding the trainer in trying to find out more about this person and if they really qualify as someone that you would like to or are qualified to work with. I use

SEABRON SKIP PAGE JR.

a health history questionnaire to find out about the new person, and to get a handle on why they think they would like to train with me. The trainer needs to know where the health risks are and what kind of risks they are dealing with. I need to know things such as if the individual ever had a heart attack, and has their doctor suggested they need to begin a workout program of some kind. If this is the case, they need a written statement from the doctor, giving authorization for me to administer a program prescription I also need to know if reporting to the doctor is going to be something that is required.

I remember assessing a client in 1995 who had been in cardiac rehab. This client's doctor wanted recorded exercise blood pressures, with before and after pulse rates. There was a particular drug that was being administered as well.

I work independently, either in client's home or with a gym as an independent contractor. I produce a document that outlines coaches' requirements for what is expected in the client-coach relationship. The document details payment requirements, notices of schedule changes, and how it is all coordinated. It details the funds that are paid up front by the client, in either a 12-workout or 1-month plan. It also describes the option of how a credit card is billed for a full three-month training cycle. This document must be signed and dated with a full reading of the document by coach and client, to make sure that there are no misunderstandings concerning the training relationship.

The actual training appointment is based on an hour, depending on the ability of the client. Certainly a beginning client's workout is not going to go a full hour due to lack of conditioning with specific precautions for injury prevention for pre-cardial and muscular adjustment to a new exercise regime. Typically a session for a new client is 40 minutes to an hour and 20 minutes to get in aerobic conditioning after a full resistance phase for persons who have passed basic core development and are beginning to advance into strength and power phase training cycles.

I do body composition analysis recorded and assessed for four-week evaluations to determine nutritional and training progress. Blood pressure readings are also evaluated if there is a known risk and if there is a concern from the client's physician. Continuing education covers the exercise prescription adjustment, and includes e-mailing workouts to clients from Ptonthenet. com, a personal training information resource. Through this service, a trainer

SEABRON SKIP PAGE JR.

can establish an account where they have a workout platform complete with pictorial workouts that can be individualized. They offer a service in which a trainer can put together workouts for clientele. When an exercise prescription is established, you can e-mail that prescription to the client so that they can get ready for their session by reading studying and visualizing movements and activities that they will be performing during the actual session. I would estimate that about 18 to 20 percent of your time will be spent on administration issues outside of the session, in an office setting.

My usual operating hours for the business are from 6 a.m. to 6 p.m. I have a specific marketing plan. I am running three to five clients, and the rest of the day is spent on product sales that I market to different segments of the population. I sell an analgesic oil for arthritis and rheumatism pain. I advocate that exercise can improve arthritic conditions that are not chronic, and that movement of any consistency improves upon quality of life. If you envision a positive life quality, it will happen when you begin to act.

All client workouts are recorded. Initially I printed workout sheets, but now I use a two-column accounting book to record workouts for each client session.

Product sales is an added profit center, so I don't have to take on clients who I really do not want to work with, or who should be referred to a trainer with different skills and abilities. I do not want to work with clients just for the money. I cannot work with everyone that crosses my path — that would not help the client or my business. Liability insurance is an expense that trainers should carry, and that I carry. Since I work independently in my business, I market and advertise on my own; however, as a contractor to a gym, I get client referrals for a $250 per month fee.

There is not a business that I can think of that is easy. The personal training business has its own particular frustrations that take time to overcome. I actually thought of getting out of it, since I struggled so hard with the ups and downs. I had begun to look at the import-export business, but that business has its own frustrations and learning curve. So I went back to personal training — my tried and true. At least this time, my concept of added product sales breathed new life into the business.

SEABRON SKIP PAGE JR.

I sell health products that I use myself, and that I believe in. I cannot sell a product unless it is of a quality that I would use for my own consumption. I would only point individuals towards this business if I felt that they were the right candidate for this job. They would have to exude passion because that is the only prerequisite that will carry you through the ups and.

I would not be able to sustain a career vision of personal training if I were not passionate about my own life, and my own philosophy of life. Fitness is a catalyst for the uplifting of consciousness, in my view. Performance is the one thing that enables me to pursue activities such as skiing, reading, writing, public presentation, and travel. These things inspire my quest for life's meaning. I am sure that people with the desire to pursue such a way of life would have to be passionate about some aspect of it that inspires them. There are more aspects of this life style that inspire me than I have time to write about here.

In my view, holism is the only aspect of life that can make you free, or at least assist you as an individual in your ascension to freedom. You have to seek it out though. As a personal trainer, you cannot preach that if that is not your own personal vision or philosophy. In answer to the question: Would I advise a young person to pursue this business? I give you the same answer that I would give a person who seeks the priesthood. It has to be part of your belief system, not to just graduate from college so that you can have a decent job, an old 20th-century concept. The truth of what you expect and want out of your life is at stake here when the question arises about becoming a priest, or when you question how deeply you want to study martial arts and how far you want to go with it. Do you really want to be a personal trainer for life, or do you want to just learn how to take care of yourself? How far do you want go in this industry? If you really want to practice, you have set to out a plan just like any other career, and work at it to progress.

This time around, I have contracted an attorney and established two business entities. Challenge Group Health and Fitness, Inc. is my mother concept for personal training. This company owns an LLC, called C Group Export Distributors, Ltd., where I do marketing for product sales with plans to export the products, some of which are being made under the name Challenge Group Health and Fitness, Inc. I am a current member in two trade associations: one in Southern California; the other in New Delhi, India. These associations are a source of continued information and for leads for companies looking to

SEABRON SKIP PAGE JR.

interchange business products and ideas, and to establish relationships. My primary interest is to export and distribute health products and services to any country throughout the world, or to any individual on this continent.

I have a current CPR certification from a job that I held in 2007, where I was stationed in Iraq on a military base. I worked as a civilian as an MWR representative, where I coordinated the operation of gym facilities; and in the soldier center, where I assisted in services for soldiers coming out of the field from combat duty. In general, I usually keep a certification and I feel it is necessary, although I must admit that sometimes these certifications lapse in time — maybe two or three years between certification.

You must make a point to stay current so you can advocate in your business literature that you are CPR certified. I think it is important to stay abreast of the techniques, because you never know when it will be of use. I have had to use it once where I had to administer it while witnessing the death of a relative. This was not business-related, but as a health and wellness practitioner, you always need to be prepared.

Not all of the experiences that I have had were necessarily grand, but they add up to the total package of assisting others with the understanding of life and health maintenance as I see it. As a personal training professional, you take all that you learn and know about your own training, and offer your philosophy to your clientele, based on basic protocols set by the industry's leading certification organizations.

Seabron obtained a Bachelor of Science degree in Business/Ebusiness in October 2005 from the University of Phoenix. He also studied with the Wellcoach Organization online in Boston, Massachusetts, in 2006. Seabron's plan for further study is to complete his ongoing education is the pursuit of a Master's of Science in Exercise Sports Science, under Health Promotion beginning in July 2008.

CASE STUDY: MARYELLEN JORDAN

ACE Certified Personal Trainer

Positively Fit Inc.

108 E. Dudley Rd

Maumee, Ohio 43537

419-893-5105

Bepositivelyfit.com

products for healthy living   fitness consulting

Maryellen Jordan has expertise in post-rehabilitation, injury recovery, sports specific training, and general fitness. She trains both competitive and recreational athletes. Maryellen is the fitness/nutrition speaker for several corporations. Serving as the strength and conditioning coach at a local girls high school, she is also on the faculty of the local college, where she teaches a personal trainer course.

I have been a personal trainer for 13 years. I have owned and operated my personal training studio for seven years. Currently I hold an American Council on Exercise (ACE) certification. It is my belief that it is a must for a personal trainer to be certified. They should seek a certification that has been recognized by the National Commission for Certifying Agencies (NCCA). The NCCA is a highly credible organization, which offers accrediting certification programs. It has certified other allied health professions such as athletic training, nursing, dietetics, and podiatry. NCCA accreditation serves as a benchmark on how organizations should conduct certification. In addition to my professional certification, I stay current with my CPR and First Aid certifications. I believe these certifications should be taught in the high schools.

I am currently the owner of a 1700-square-foot personal training studio. I also am contracted with a local private high school as the strength and conditioning coach. I am contracted out by a corporate health service company as an expert in exercise. I conduct seminars at local organizations, businesses, and in my studio.

CASE STUDY: MARYELLEN JORDAN

I keep up on current trends by having memberships to several professional organizations. I also attend training conventions and workshops. I supplement this by purchasing educational materials, and reading literature and research papers. I spend at least an hour per day on continuing my education as a personal trainer.

I have health screenings with clients, which includes a medical history form clients fill out along with the Physical Activity Readiness Questionnaire (PARQ) form. If necessary, we get a release from the client's doctor. After we have completed these health forms, the clients will sign a contract that gives a 100 percent money back guarantee on weight loss. They have to sign a contract before the training begins.

I keep the following hours of operation:

6 a.m.–7 p.m.   Monday–Friday

8 a.m.–3 p.m.   Saturday

Closed on Sundays

I personal train 30 to 35 hours a week. I spend three to five hours the rest of the week on marketing, office work, selling, and promoting the business.

In the Toledo area, the rates for a personal trainer range between $20 and $60 per hour. All my trainers have their own liability insurance along with the liability insurance I carry for the studio.

This has been a very good profession for me. I have been extremely satisfied, therefore I have been able to stay in this business and raise a family for more than ten years. I love the flexibility I had when my children where young. My complaints would be that I have no paid vacation or sick pay. Also, if the studio closes due to bad weather, I cannot train, giving me no income for that day. Health insurance is expensive since I am self-employed.

The most important attributes as a trainer are compassion and a genuine concern that your clients reach their goals. Once you get your certification, do not stop acquiring the knowledge and skills you need to help your clients reach their goals. Invest time and money in education and marketing skills. Learn how to sell yourself and what you have to offer. Marketing and sales are two of the most important things that a trainer needs to learn about.

CASE STUDY: MARYELLEN JORDAN

CASE STUDY: LINDSAY VASTOLA

Lindsay Vastola

Certified Fitness Trainer, ISSA

Founder and Owner, Body Project LLC

609-336-0108

lindsay@mybodyproject.com

www.mybodyproject.com

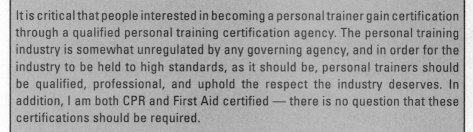

Serving Princeton, New Jersey and surrounding areas

I was certified as a fitness trainer in January 2007 through International Sports Sciences Association (ISSA).

It is critical that people interested in becoming a personal trainer gain certification through a qualified personal training certification agency. The personal training industry is somewhat unregulated by any governing agency, and in order for the industry to be held to high standards, as it should be, personal trainers should be qualified, professional, and uphold the respect the industry deserves. In addition, I am both CPR and First Aid certified — there is no question that these certifications should be required.

I recommend that someone considering a career in personal training have a college degree (at least associate's or bachelor's). It is also important that personal trainers continually educate themselves through courses offered at colleges and universities or by certifying agencies and industry leaders. I have a Bachelor of Arts from American University in Washington, DC.

I am the founder and owner of an at-home and online personal training company, Body Project LLC. My background in fitness training began more than ten years ago as an assistant in the physical therapy and rehabilitation center, HealthSouth. I worked with athletes and rehabilitation patients of all ages for post-surgery or post-injury physical therapy. After three years with HealthSouth, I worked as an assistant athletic trainer at American University for four years. I have worked with high school, NCAA Division I, and semi-pro athletes, and have personally been involved in weight training and sports conditioning through participation in basketball, volleyball, cheerleading, and rugby. Since certified as a fitness trainer, I have trained men and women ages 18 to 80 as well high school athletic teams.

CASE STUDY: LINDSAY VASTOLA

It is a priority to keep up-to-date with industry trends, research, and techniques through different media. I attend industry seminars that offer the opportunity to meet other industry professionals and learn what they are doing in their own practice. I constantly read or subscribe to online and print publications including PFP publications (**www.fit-pro.com**), *Club Solutions* magazine, and the *National Journal of Health Promotions*. I also frequent **NIH.gov** and other health agencies who offer updates on health studies. It is also important to network with other fitness and health professionals. The industry is constantly evolving, so it is important to keep up with the change.

I require a doctor's release from high-risk clients (in particular, those over 55, with high blood-pressure or cholesterol, diabetes, stroke, heart conditions, or any client who has had major surgery). I also communicate with all of my clients' doctors to inform them of the type of program the patient is following — both nutrition and exercise. By informing the doctor of a client's fitness routine, the doctor can closely monitor changes in follow-up check-ups, blood work, overall health, or current health conditions. My goal is to create a relationship with my clients' doctors in order to provide the client with the most optimal and comprehensive healthcare program. I also feel liability insurance is important and my insurance is $1 million per incident, $3 million aggregate.

All of my clients are required to sign a contract. The contract includes a waiver of liability and outlines scheduling, payment, and cancellation policies. I also require a separate "contract" for my client, called "Get the most out of your Body Project," which outlines the guidelines and requests that will help ensure they receive the most effective workouts and ensure the safety of all parties. These guidelines include requesting that phones and pagers are off during our time, and that, pets and children are cared for; appropriate exercise clothing; instructions on how to set up the workout space for optimum safety, and encouraging clients to inform me if they feel any discomfort or uneasiness.

My first session of the day is 6 a.m., and the last is 8 p.m., Monday thru Friday, and Saturdays, 6 a.m. to 12:30 p.m. I typically work about 40 to 60 hours per week. Approximately 70 percent of total working time is with clients; 20 percent is spent on administration including accounting, networking events, marketing, sales, and client maintenance duties (tracking progress, sending newsletters to clients and prospects). Approximately 10 percent is spent on continuing education, seminars, reading industry, or business news.

CASE STUDY: LINDSAY VASTOLA

Depending on the location, anywhere from $55 to $75+ per hour would be a fair hourly charge for a new personal trainer, competitive with the market (this rate is based on the Northeast — New Jersey, New York, Pennsylvania).

Each of my clients is provided with a goal and progress tracking "Toolkit" which includes a time line of goals (body fat percentage, overall weight, heart rate monitoring, flexibility, endurance, etc.). They are also given a food and exercise log for which they are accountable. Updated "toolkits" are e-mailed to them every two weeks after weight assessments. Other progress tracking, including body measurements and other fitness assessments, are done on a monthly basis to keep them accountable to their goals.

Being a personal trainer is perhaps one of the most satisfying and rewarding careers. It is empowering to help people attain lifelong goals, giving them the power to embrace change and enjoy life, and it has given me the opportunity and flexibility to run my own successful business.

If someone genuinely wants to help others help themselves, a career as a personal trainer is ideal. The person must be passionate about health and fitness and hold themselves accountable for their own health, the same as they expect from their clients. It is a privilege to be a part of the fitness industry and the individual should be prepared to represent the industry in the most professional way possible. Some of the mot important attributes of a personal trainer are compassion, confidence, integrity, assertiveness, honesty, and accountability.

The most valuable advice would be to surround yourself with other successful personal trainers and industry professionals. Always be reading and educating yourself — industry publications, current events, and personal and professional development books. Also, always go the extra mile for your clients. They instill a great deal of trust in you and you will differentiate yourself from the next trainer; fostering a successful business. Birthday cards, thank you cards, an occasional phone call to keep them motivated, get them water when they need it, or send them a health article that they might be interested in — the little things really go a long way in developing outstanding and long-lasting relationships.

The ideal type of business model for a personal trainer depends on long-term business goals. An independent personal trainer just starting his or her business may be best off as a sole proprietor. In my case, I am a single-member LLC.

CASE STUDY: LINDSAY VASTOLA

As my company grows, incorporating may be advantageous for tax and legal purposes. Only in the circumstances where both parties are in full agreement, signed and agreed upon in a lawyer-reviewed contract, would a partnership be a fitting business model.

Since working independently, I am solely responsible, even in the case of an emergency. I believe that once a client begins a relationship with a personal trainer, that trainer should be responsible for all client contact. Personal training is a business of creating personal relationships — not transactions.

It is important for a personal trainer to treat each client as a unique individual — as though that person is your only client, not just a number. Never stop educating yourself on health, fitness, business, current events, and personal and professional development.

CASE STUDY: GARETH PHILLIPS

Gareth Phillips

Personal Trainer B. Sc. (Hons), MBA

BodyRestored.com

Blog: **www.bodyrestored.com/blog/blog.html**

Books: **stores.lulu.com/bodyrestored**

e-mail: garethphillips@bodyrestored.com

I have been a personal trainer since 2003. This is a second career for me. I had come back from a telecoms project in India to my home in Alpharetta, Georgia, and decided I did not want to do projects like that again. So I retired, did nothing for a while, got into bad habits, until finally my wife told me I was not going to live long if I did not start working again.

She suggested becoming a personal trainer because I have exercised and played sports pretty much my whole adult life. It has turned out to be a good decision. I had many years of experience with sports and training plus my first degree was in Biological Science, so I understood the basics of muscle and skeletal physiology. I meet interesting people, help them with serious issues and I benefit through a healthy, active, get-up-early life style. I am a personal trainer alone and in a commercial gym.

When I began my new career, I studied for the ACE qualification as a personal trainer and passed the first time. I contacted Bally's and they offered me a job as a personal trainer. Later, I added other qualifications and opened a train-at-home business. To do this, I incorporated as Gareth Phillips Communications Inc.

Early in 2007, I started my Web site, **www.bodyrestored.com**, as a means to share my reading with anyone who has the same interests. My training clients have a variety of medical and injury issues which gives me an incentive to keep on learning. At the moment asthma and diabetes are subjects I spend a lot of time on.

I have the following certifications: ACSM Personal Trainer, ACE Clinical Exercise Specialist and ACE Lifestyle and Weight Management Trainer.

CASE STUDY: GARETH PHILLIPS

I recommend that other professionals entering the personal training field also gain certification. I am certified in CPR and believe that it is a vital qualification. I have an MBA. I feel that other professionals should at least have a bachelor's degree in a relevant topic to fitness.

I keep up with the current trends by reading ACSM's health and fitness journal, *ACSM Fit Society, ACSM Certified News, ACE Fitness Matters, NSCA Performance Training Journal. OnFitness Magazine, Tufts Health & Nutrition Newsletter,* and *PFP Magazine.* The *New York Times* and *Wall Street Journal* both have a steady stream of interesting fitness and health articles. As I study and renew my certifications, it provides me a wealth new of information. Lastly, mainly for amusement, I check T-Nation once a week.

When I get a new client, I always have them complete a PAR-Q and if that brings up any issues I ask them to get a note from their doctor before we start working out. As a self-employed trainer, I do not have written contracts with clients, but I have all clients sign an Informed Consent and a Waiver of Liability. When I train clients at a commercial gym, that gym always has written contracts. I do record keeping with the clients that includes status of health and injury issues, exercises contra-indicated for them or not used in light of experience, and maximum capability in key exercises.

My regular hours of working with clients is 5 a.m. to 1 p.m. I work about 40 hours a week, taking everything into account. Here is a break down of my time:

With Clients	80%
Administration	5% (includes Web-site updates)
Education	15%

A fair charge as a personal trainer depends on the area, but in Georgia about $25 to $40 per hour (more expensive closer to Atlanta). I personally carry liability insurance due to the type of work. Incorporation is the safest if you have, or might have in the future, any serious assets. I have an S-corp, which allows business losses to flow through to personal taxation.

I find that being a personal trainer is very pleasant and for me a healthy, active life style. I do not know if I can recommend this career for everyone; it really depends on the individual. There are some things that I believe a trainer must

CASE STUDY: GARETH PHILLIPS

have to be successful, such as being empathetic, knowledgeable, and positive. If I had one piece of advice to give to new trainers it would be learn, learn, learn and then market hard. The two most important assets that a personal trainer has got to have is a mind for marketing and an awesome reputation.

CASE STUDY: DAN BIALIK

Dan Bialik

Dan's Health & Fitness

danshealth.dan4fitness.com

dan4fitness@aol.com

I perform free online consultations via my Web site.

I have been a personal trainer for nine years. I have been certified by NAHF, IFA, and Expert Training. I recommend that other trainers get certified mainly for their own confidence. I recommend that new trainers try to get as much information as they can get their hands on. A college degree would probably help them a lot. I was CPR certified in 1998 and I believe it is important for all trainers.

I was self-employed as a personal trainer. Now, I do free consultations online. I have trained with weights since 1973. I have trained in the martial arts since 1974. I keep up with trends by reading everything I can on the Internet.

When I was a trainer, I did verbal consultations before starting. I never trained anyone I considered in risky health. If I had, I would request a doctor's release.

CASE STUDY: DAN BIALIK

I never required a contract as a personal trainer. I do not know what the rates are now, but when I was a trainer I charged $20, which was probably too cheap.

As a trainer, I did things manually. If I was successful, I would use online tracking software. I had liability insurance my last professional year in 2006. I was a trainer because I loved helping people. I hated selling and asking for their money, which is part of the job. I recommend that a person become a personal trainer if they have the ability to sell themselves to their clients. I was very knowledgeable, but not successful, so I would say that a successful trainer needs to be aggressive. If you are going to go into this field, you need to know your stuff and do your homework! If I had to do it over, I wish I could have hooked up with a partner who was more into aerobics training. I was a sole proprietor.

CASE STUDY: BRANDON JENKINS

Brandon Jenkins

Born Again Fitness LLC

BornAgainFitness.com

208-514-8384

Bjenkins@bornagainfitness.com

I have been a personal trainer for ten years. I am an International Fitness Professionals Association (IFPA) personal trainer, National Association of Sports Medicine (NASM) personal trainer, and IFPA bodybuilding instructor. I recommend other personal trainers also get certifications. In addition, I have a college education and recommend that other trainers get at least a bachelor's degree, if not a master's degree when deciding to become a personal trainer. I am

CASE STUDY: BRANDON JENKINS

CPR and First Aid certified, and I believe that other trainers should do the same.

I have trained at the YMCA, but have been independent for last three years. I have a background in bodybuilding and sports nutrition. I keep up with what is going on in the world of fitness by going to fitness seminars, reading periodicals, and getting new certifications.

When I get a new client, I do a health screening that includes a release from their doctor. In addition, I create a written contract with the client. For each client I chart the weight used, reps, how long to keep them on this workout, resting heart rate, weight, and body fat percentage measurements.

My hours are Monday thru Saturday 5 a.m. to 7 p.m. I work about 30 to 40 hours a week and, of that time, 75 percent is working with the clients. I believe that $40 an hour is a fair fee, though this can fluctuate depending on where you live. I carry liability insurance. I prefer to be a sole proprietor of my business. You must provide great customer service, and always deliver what you promise.

I reside in Idaho where I am a personal trainer and fitness coach. I also work with student athletes. I am pursuing my master's degree at Boise State where I hope to become a strength and conditioning coach in the future.

CASE STUDY: ANTONIO EVANS

Antonio Evans

ReShape Fitness, LLC

P.O. Box 1636

Huntersville, NC 28070

Phone: 704-529-2950

E-mail: Info@reshapefitness.net

Web Site: **www.reshapefitness.net**

ReShape Fitness, LLC is a mobile fitness service providing in-home training and fitness boot camps in the Charlotte, North Carolina area. ReShape Fitness's philosophy

CASE STUDY: ANTONIO EVANS

is to educate and empower our clients to achieve mental and physical transformation through fitness.

I have been a personal trainer for the past eight years. I hold certifications with the National Academy of Sports Medicine-Certified Personal Trainer CPT, GMP Fitness-Certified Golf Conditioning Specialist, and Fitour-Certified Bootcamp Instructor. I highly recommend obtaining a national certification when entering the fitness industry. I have a Bachelor of Science Degree in Exercise Science from the University of South Carolina in Aiken. For someone entering the personal training industry, I recommend at least a bachelor' degree along with national certification. I have CPR and First Aid certification, and I think they are very important for all personal trainers.

I am self-employed and I do contract work as well. I work with many different populations of people in many different settings. I have worked with cardiac rehab patients and CEO's of major corporations, so my experience is very rewarding. Now, I specialize in fitness boot camps, and in-home clients. I also do fitness workshops for local universities and organizations. I keep current on fitness trends by attending annual fitness conferences and watching weekly fitness videos from some of the best in the fitness industry. I always want to be on the cutting edge of research and information to better serve my clients.

I require a fitness evaluation for all new clients and pending on the individual, I may require a doctor's release form. I do not require written contracts with all my clients. I chart all their workouts, keep records of their weight and body fat measurements. This is the road map to get them where they want to go.

I am available from 5 a.m. to 7 p.m. Monday thru Friday and by appointment on Saturday. I am averaging 40 to 50 hours per week, of work. 90 percent of which is spent with my clients. I would say fees vary based on their region, but $40 to $60 per hour is a great start. I carry liability insurance and am a sole proprietor. .

Being a fitness professional is a very rewarding career. There are challenges in this field as in any other field, but I love what I do, so the good always out weigh the bad. I would highly recommend personal training as a career for those who are passionate about helping people. It is important that they have a desire to help, good listening skills, business skills, and are knowledgeable, and trustworthy. I would encourage them to find someone that is already successful and learn as much as you can from them. The two most important things for a personal trainer are a knack for business skills and knowledge of exercise physiology.

CASE STUDY: DAN DEFIGIO

Dan DeFigio

defigio@gettingfit.com

I have been a personal trainer since 1993.
I have the following certifications:

Certified personal trainer through ACE, NFPT, IFPA

American Council on Exercise faculty

Continuing education provider for NSCA, ACSM

Certified Sports Nutrition Counselor NFPT, IFPA

Advanced Sports Nutrition Specialist NFPT

Certified Post-Rehab Conditioning Specialist

State Representative, NFPT

Continuing Education Specialist

I recommend that others entering the personal trainer field also get certifications. In addition I am CPR and First Aid certified and recommend that trainers have these as well. I am currently working on my Master's Degree in Rehabilitative Science.

I own a large health and fitness company based in Nashville, Tennessee. I have 12 professionals who work for me, and we offer personal fitness training, physical therapy, nutrition counseling, and corporate wellness programs. Since 1993, I have worked with hundreds of individuals hands-on, hosted my own fitness television show, and have been featured in numerous magazines and publications. My personal day-to-day practice consists primarily of post-injury clients and other special populations. I teach workshops for other trainers' continuing education requirements. You can read more at **www.gettingfit.com** if you would like more details. I am the owner and of sole-proprietor of Basics and Beyond, which is an LLC. We carry liability insurance.

CASE STUDY: DAN DEFIGIO

In order to stay current on what is going on in the fitness industry I read professional journals and publications, do Internet research, read industry newsletters, attend live workshops, and watch instructional DVDs.

When a new client comes in to meet with us, we use a detailed health history interview and questionnaire. In special circumstances, you may ask for a release from the client's doctor. We do not have contracts or packages. Each client keeps food journals, has daily workout journals, and homework.

My personal schedule runs from 7:30 a.m. to about 7:30 p.m. I work 20 to 30 hours per week hands-on with clients, 20 to 30 hours per week being a boss. The break down of my time is 50 percent clients, 20 percent administration, 20 percent marketing and business growth, 10 percent research and education. In Nashville, $40 to $45 per hour would be reasonable for a new trainer.

I am very satisfied with my choice of being a personal trainer. I recommend that people should become a trainer if they have a passion for helping people and teaching.

CASE STUDY: AIMEE MARSHALL

I have been a personal trainer for 18 years. I am certified through AFAA. I highly recommend other trainers also become certified. I have a Bachelor's Degree in Organizational Management. I highly recommend accredited certification as well as having a college education. I am certified in CPR and recommend other trainers do the same.

CASE STUDY: AIMEE MARSHALL

I work in a gym as an independent contractor, at home, and at a health club as an employee. I was an All-Western Massachusetts and All-State cross country runner and track and field. I was recruited to Southeastern Massachusetts University to run for their team. I was also a coach for the local high school in both departments. In order to stay on top of what is going on in fitness, I attend workshops three to four times a year.

I do an assessment with new clients, and if they have medical issues or risks I receive a medical clearance from their doctor. I do a contract with the client before we begin working out. I make my own charts and filing system to keep up with my clients.

My hours are whenever the gym is open, within reason. I work about 60 to 70 hours a week. The break down of my time is 70 percent with clients, 10 percent administration work, and 20 percent continuing education. I don't need to market due to many word-of-mouth referrals and by acquiring clients through teaching classes. Reasonable fees depend on the state and the city. In my area, $35 to $40 per hour would be the most people would pay. My employer carries insurance for me, but I also carry my own liability insurance.

I do recommend personal trainer as a career if you are prepared to work. A personal trainer should have the following characteristics to be successful: kindness, caring, flexibility, and knowing when to push or back off. My advice is to stay focused on your journey, your client, and to stay educated and up to date on all fitness levels. The two must important aspects are getting enthusiastic and having an excellent work ethic

Deciding what type of business structure to set up it will depend on your financial income and backing that is available to you, if you want time off and if you want to share your space and money.

Tip

Drink plenty of water. Most people will not start drinking water until their bodies have already become dehydrated. Reach for the H$_2$0 before you feel thirsty to avoid dehydration.

Appendix B: What Supplies/ Forms Do I Need?

You must adhere to all reporting and payment schedules set by the IRS. This may vary according to the type of legal structure you have selected for your business. Here is the calendar for a sole proprietorship and the forms you will need to file. This is the schedule that you are most likely to use as a personal trainer. The ones in italics will only apply if you have employees. You can find a full tax calendar at **http://www.irs.gov/businesses/small/ article/0,,id=104684,00.html**.

Here are some dates you should be aware of and the forms you will need to fill out and send to the IRS. These dates as based upon a sole proprietor structure.

January

- ⫟ 15 Pay the final installment of your 2007 estimated tax. Use Form 1040-ES.

- ⫟ 31 File Forms 940, 941, 943, 944 and/or 945, if you did not deposit all taxes when due. File Form 720 for the 4th quarter of 2007. Furnish Forms 1098, 1099 and W-2G to recipients for certain payments made during previous year.

February

Ⓨ 15 File information returns (Forms 1098, 1099 and W-2G) for certain payments made during 2007.

April

Ⓨ 15 File Form 1040, 1040-A, or 1040-EZ and pay any tax due. Pay the first installment of your estimated tax for the current year.

Ⓨ 15 File Form 941 if you did not deposit all taxes when due.

June

Ⓨ 15 Make a payment of your current year estimated tax.

September

Ⓨ 15 Make a payment of your current years estimated tax.

October

Ⓨ 17 If you filed a Form 4868 requesting an automatic 6-month extension of time to file, file a previous calendar year return (Form 1040, 1040-A or 1040-EZ).

Ⓨ 15 File Form 941 if you did not deposit all taxes when due.

Now this may seem overwhelming, but not all of these forms will apply to you if you do not have employees or utilize independent contractors.

If you have employees here are some other dates you need to consider. Every Wednesday and Friday you will have to Deposit Payroll tax for payments if the semiweekly deposit rule applies. You will have to make deposits on the 15th if the monthly rule applies for employees. Every last day of the month you must File Form 730 and pay the tax on wagers accepted the previous month.

Here are some additional tax dates you should be aware of.

January

   Y 15 Secure a new Form W-4 from employees claiming "exempt" during previous year. Deposit Payroll tax for January if the monthly deposit rule applies. Begin withholding income tax from employees who claimed exemption from withholding in 2007 but did not submit a new Form W-4 on February 16th.

   Y Deposit FUTA tax owed through Dec if $500 or less

February

   Y 28/29 File Form W-3, "Transmittal of Wage and Tax Statements."

   Y Copy A of all Forms W-2 you issued in previous year.

April

   Y 15 Partnerships: File a previous calendar year return (Form

1065 or 1065-B). Provide each partner with a copy of Sch. K-1.

Y Deposit FUTA (unemployment tax) owed through March if more than $500.

July

Y Deposit FUTA tax owed through June if more than $500.

October

Y Deposit FUTA tax owed through September if more than $500.

If your fiscal year does not follow the calendar year then income tax is due on the fifteenth day of the fourth month after the end of your tax year.

This of course is a more complicated set of taxes and dates and forms. This is something to consider BEFORE you set up a partnership or hire employees because you might be forced to hire an accountant, and your bookkeeping duties will jump dramatically. So, just when you did not think things could get any more difficult, consider the tax schedule for employees.

When you decide to become a small-business owner and start your own personal training business, you take on a lot of responsibility. The day you decide to hire employees things will change dramatically. First is that you can no longer just use your social security number, you must get a federal EIN.

You must file your employee's federal, state, and local taxes. There is a certain amount of taxes you must withhold from your employees' paychecks.

If your fiscal year does not follow the calendar year, income tax is due on the fifteenth day of the fourth month after the end of your tax year.

Schedule SE is due the same day as income tax (Form 1040).

Estimated Tax (1040ES) is due on the fifteenth day of the fourth, sixth and ninth months of the tax year and the 15th day of the 1st month after the end of your tax year.

This, of course, is a more complicated set of taxes, dates, and forms. This is something to consider before you set up a partnership, because you might be forced to hire an accountant, and your bookkeeping duties will increase dramatically. So, just when you did not think things could get any more difficult, consider the tax schedule for employees.

When you decide to become a small-business owner and start your own personal training business, you take on much responsibility. The day you decide to hire employees, things will change dramatically, beginning with no longer being able to use your Social Security number — you must get a federal EIN.

You must file your employees' federal, state, and local taxes. There are a certain amount of taxes you must withhold from your employees' paychecks. Here is a list of typical taxes you will be responsible for as an employer:

- Federal income tax withholding
- Social Security and Medicare taxes
- Federal Unemployment Tax Act (FUTA)
- Federal income taxes/Social Security and Medicare taxes

In order to figure out how much you must withhold for federal taxes on your employee, refer to the employee's Form W-4. For help navigating this form, refer to Publication 15, Employer's Tax Guide, and Publication 15-A, and the Employer's Supplemental Tax Guide.

www.irs.gov/pub/irs-pdf/fw4.pdf

www.irs.gov/pub/irs-pdf/p15.pdf

For additional resources regarding taxes, please use the free resources that the IRS offers:

The Small Business Resource Guide, available at **www.irs.gov/ smallbiz**, or by calling 800-829-3676.

Other I.R.S. forms, publications, and instructions, call 800-829-3676.

Tax Related Questions, call 800-829-4933.

TeleTax Topics, call 800-829-4477.

Refund Information, call 800-829-829-4477, or 800-829-1954, for a live customer service representative.

Bibliography

Sitarz, D. *Sole Proprietorship, Small Business Start Up Kit*. 2nd Ed. Carbondale: Nova, 2007.

Pinson, L. & J. Jinnett, *Steps to Small Business Start Up, Everything You Need to Know to Turn Your Idea into a Successful Business*. Chicago: Kaplan, 2006.

Editors of Socrates, *Business Plan Book, Advice From the Experts*. Chicago: Socrates, 2006.

BPlans.com **www.bplans.com/sample_business_plans/Wedding_and_Event_Planning_Business_Plans/Wedding_Consultant_Business_Plan/executive_summary_fc.cfm**

Tip

Come up with a list of small goals. The easier the goal is to reach, the more goals that will be reached. Try working out for three 10-minute sessions instead of one long 30-minute session.

Author Biography

John N. Peragine

John N Peragine, Ph.D., is a freelance writer and classical musician. John holds a B.S. in psychology from Appalachian State University. John is the author of the books *365 Low or No Cost Workplace Teambuilding Activities* and *How to Open & Operate* *a Financially Successful Wedding Planning and Consultant Business.* When John is not writing, he plays the piccolo in the Western Piedmont Symphony.

Glossary

AEROBICS or AEROBIC EXERCISE: Any exercise that uses large muscle groups and depends mainly on the oxygen from the blood. The oxygen is used as fuel to energize the working muscles of the body. Examples are endurance activities such as running, cycling and swimming. Literally meaning "with oxygen."

ANAEROBIC EXERCISE: An intense or fast paced activity usually done for short periods of time where you become breathless because oxygen cannot be processed quickly enough. Examples are weight lifting and sprinting. Literally meaning "without oxygen."

ASTHMA, EXERCISE-INDUCED: A blockage of airways during strenuous activity hat can cause a shortness of breath within a few minutes of beginning to exercise. This can be effectively remedied with inhalers prescribed by a doctor.

BARBELL: A piece of exercise equipment used in weight training. This piece of equipment consists of a single steel bar. Weighted plates can be added to the end of the bar allowing the lifter to reach the desired total weight. The weighted plates are secured on the end of the bar to prevent injuries during exercise.

BICEP MUSCLE: Located on the upper arm, this muscle allows the elbow to flex and the forearm to rotate.

BIOMECHANICS: The study of application and mathematical methods of mechanics. Used to learn about the movement of the human body.

BODYBUILDING: Can be a competitive sport or athletic hobby where a trainee tries to achieve maximum muscular build.

BODY FAT: Normally expressed as a percentage, it is the total weight of a person's fat divided by the person's weight. This percentage reflects a person's essential fat and storage fat.

BODYPART: This is in reference to different groups of muscles. Often when exercising, routines are split up by exercising different groups of muscles on different days. Some people choose to do all over body workouts.

BURN: A reaction due to the occurrence of lactic acid in the tissues causing a burning feeling in the specific muscles being exercised. This feeling is often welcomed by trainees as this means you are effectively working the muscle group.

BURNOUT: When a person becomes bored with their workout routine or when they have exercised to the point of overtraining.

CARDIO: Often referring to the heart. Also referring to cardiovascular or aerobic exercise.

CONCENTRIC CONTRACTION: A muscle contraction allowing muscles to shorten and generate force. An example would be pulling the weight up during bicep curls.

COOL DOWN: A gradual slowing at the end of exercise, allowing your body temperature, heart rate, and blood pressure to return to normal slowly and safely.

DELTOIDS: The three-part muscle group of the shoulder. Includes the anterior, middle, and posterior. This muscle is also known as the "Delts."

DOMS (Delayed Onset Muscular Soreness): Pain often felt 24-72 hours after strenuous exercise thought to be caused by small tears in the muscle, causing stiffness and loss of strength.

DUMBBELLS: A type of free weight. A piece of weight training equipment held in one hand. Can be an adjustable or fixed weight.

ECCENTRIC CONTRACTION: A muscle contraction allowing muscles to elongate while it is under tension. An example would be lowering the weight down during bicep curls.

ELECTROLYTES: A substance consisting of free ions. Electrolytes are often lost as the body sweats. Often found in sports drinks to help a dehydrated body replenish its water and electrolyte levels. After extremely strenuous exercise the consumption of sports drinks containing electrolytes is often recommended, however, the body has the ability to replenish its own electrolytes naturally.

EXTENSION: During exercise, when a joint is straightened, such as in a leg extension.

EXERCISE: Activity of the body. Helps to maintain overall bodily fitness and health. Can also refer to a specific set of movements.

EZ CURL BAR or BENT BAR: A type of barbell that is bent allowing a more comfortable grip on the bar. Can help to prevent pain in the wrists and elbows often felt in a straight barbell.

FLEXIBILITY: Having the ability to move or bend the body easily without pain or stiffness.

FLOW: Referring to the continuous movement during exercise.

FOCUS: The cognitive process of concentrating all your attention on one element of your environment. During exercise, refers to putting all of your attention into working one specific muscle group and everything that involves the exercise of this group.

FULL RANGE OF MOTION: Having the ability to move a muscle or joint in all ways physically possible, compared to only being able to move the muscle or joint partially in a certain direction or movement.

GETTING CUT: A term referring to achieving muscle tone and overall fitness through exercise and diet.

GETTING RIPPED: A term referring to achieving extreme muscle tone and definition through weight training and dieting.

GLUTEUS MAXIMUS (Glutes, butt, bottom, and rear): The largest of the three gluteal muscles forming the shape of the buttock.

GLYCOGEN: Stores short-term energy in the body. The body can only hold a certain amount of this chemical and once the levels have depleted athletes can experience extreme fatigue. This is often referred to as "hitting the wall." This phenomenon occurs mostly in extremely long distance running, but can be delayed by the intake of carbohydrates before the exercise.

GRIP: The force or pressure on an object that is applied by a person's hands and fingers. In exercise, a person with a strong grip often has more strength.

HAMSTRINGS: Refers to the muscle behind the thigh. Plays an important role in walking, running, and jumping.

HEART RATE, AMBIENT: The rate that the heart beats when you are awake, but not exercising.

HEART RATE, MAXIMUM (MHR): The highest number of times that a heart can beat in one minute or the highest rate that a person could achieve during extreme exercise.

HEART RATE, RECOVERY: The amount of time that it takes for the heart to return to its normal rate after exercise.

HEART RATE, RESERVE: The difference between the maximum and resting heart rate.

HEART RATE, RESTING (RHR): The rate that the heartbeats when the body is completely at rest. Should be taken first thing in the morning, before you get out of bed.

HEART RATE, TARGET (THR): The desired rate of the heart to be reached during aerobic exercise. Reaching this rate during a workout is beneficial for the heart.

HEART RATE, TARGET ZONES: Depends on the number of heart beats in one minute. The different zones allow for different levels of intensity during the workout.

HEART RATE CALCULATIONS: Usually calculated by the number of beats in one minute. Can be measured by using multiple methods, including the taking of the pulse rate, with a stethoscope, or an having an EKG done at a doctor's office.

HIGH REPS: In weight training, where the same muscle is worked the same amount of times for an extended number of repetitions. This can be done for a multitude of reasons such as practice, warm-up, increased muscle tone, or weight loss or gain.

HIT (high-intensity training): A form of strength training where exercise is done in brief, but intense spurts. Some believe that HIT is more effective for size and strength building.

INTENSITY: The level of energy put into a workout.

ISOKINETIC CONTRACTION: When a muscle contracts and shortens at a constant speed.

ISOLATION: In fitness, refers to concentrating on one specific muscle group in a workout.

ISOMETRIC CONTRACTION: When a muscle contract and does not shorten, giving no movement.

ISOTONIC CONTRACTION: When a muscle contracts and shortens, giving movement.

INTERVALS: Refers to exercise where a person alternates between extremely high intense workouts followed by periods of low activity workouts.

KETTLEBELLS: A weighted ball that has the appearance of a cannonball with a handle.

KILOMETER: A unit of measurement used often in distance running. Uses the abbreviation Km. One kilometer is equal to 1000 meters.

KINESIOLOGY: The study of how humans move.

LACTIC ACID: A chemical compound that is created in the muscles during intense workouts. This allows energy levels to be maintained so that the workout can continue.

LATISSIMUS DORSI or LATS: A large muscle on the back that stretches from under the armpit down to the gluteus. Creates the "V" shape of the back.

LIGAMENT: A short band of connective tissue. Connects bones to other bones forming joints.

LOW REPS: In weight training, where the same muscle is worked the same amount of time for short intervals.

MAX REP or SINGLES: In reference to weightlifting, when heavy single repetition sets are used.

MET (Metabolic Equivalent): Used to calculate the intensity of a workout, is the ratio of the metabolic rate to the resting metabolic rate.

MULTI-SET: A series of exercises performed continuously with short pauses between sets.

MUSCLE SORENESS: Pain felt in the muscles after exercise, usually felt 24 to 72 hours after the workout, thought to be caused by tears in the muscle.

NUTRITION: Food that is necessary to sustain life.

OLYMPIC BAR and PLATES: A type of barbell used in competition and training. Must have rotating ends to keep the bar from injuring the lifters arms and wrists.

OLYMPIC LIFTING: The weightlifting sport of the Olympic Games.

OVERTRAINING: When a person becomes bored with their workout routine or when they have exercised to the point of burnout.

PACE: The speed in which a workout progresses.

PECTORALS or PECS: The muscles that run across the top of the chest.

PERSONAL TRAINER: A professional that helps clients with overall fitness. Usually hired for a fee.

POWERLIFTING: A weightlifting sport that consists of the bench press, the squat, and the deadlift.

PR (Personal Record): Refers to someone's personal best or high during a workout.

PUMP: Following a weightlifting session, a tight sensation of the muscle caused by the engorgement of blood.

PUMPING IRON: A term meaning lifting weights.

QUADRICEPS or QUADS: The four-part muscle group on the front of the thighs.

RACE WALK: A long-distance track and field sport. Race walking is often referred to as speed walking in the fitness industry, but the actual sport is governed by specific rules.

REPETITION or REP: The number of times that you do an exercise within a set. For example, if you do two sets of ten repetitions, then you would do the exercise ten times, take a short pause, and then do another set of ten.

RHYTHM: Describes the flow or pace of the workout.

RICE: A common treatment for injuries as the result of exercise. The acronym stands for Rest, Ice, Compression, and Elevation.

ROTATOR CUFF: The term given to the group of muscles and tendons that make up the shoulder.

SANDBAGS: In weight training, refers to bags that are filled with sand and carried to build strength.

SERRATUS: Refers to the three-tiered muscle group in the central part of the body.

SET: The number of times that you do an exercise. Refer to repetition for more information.

SHIN SPLINTS: A term for pain located in the shin.

SINGLE-SET TRAINING: In weight training, where a lifter does a single set of the exercise at an extreme weight limit.

SLED PULLING: A workout where a heavy-weighted object is pulled for a distance.

SMITH PRESS: Training equipment that contains a bar that is easily guided by accuracy rods and bearings.

SPLIT WORKOUT: A workout that is divided into two or more body parts, allowing different muscle groups to be worked on different days.

SPOT: The act of standing close by in a supportive way as a co-lifter attempts heavy lifting. Used as a safety measure in case the lifter is unable to get the weight into a starting position or needs assistance lowering the weight.

SPOTTER: Someone who spots a co-lifter.

SPRAIN: An injury to a ligament.

STONE LIFTING: Cement balls used to train for or compete in competitions.

STRAIN: An injury to a muscle or tendon.

STRETCHING, BALLISTIC: Known as a dangerous method of stretching because of the possibility of muscles tears, involves bouncing into a stretch.

STRETCHING, STATIC: Known as the safest method of stretching, involves reaching to a point on the body until you are unable to reach any further, and then holding this position.

STROKE VOLUME: The amount of blood that is pumped per contraction of the heart.

STRONGMAN EVENTS: Competitions featuring events that test a competitor's strength and endurance.

SUPERSET: When you combine 2 different sets of exercises, one fallowed by the other.

SUPPLEMENTS: Substances taken by athletes to aid in different bodily processes.

TENDINITIS: Sometimes called tendinopathy, refers to microscopic tears in the muscle as a result of the muscle being overused.

TENDON: A band of tissues that connect a muscle to a bone.

TORSO: Refers to muscles located in the trunk or midsection of a body.

TRAINING LOG: A journal that trainers often use to keep personal notes regarding their progress.

TRICEPS or TR: A three-part muscle located on the back of the upper arm.

TRI-SETS: When three sets of an exercise are done consecutively.

URINE: Waste that is exited through the body in liquid form.

VO2 MAX: The maximum amount of oxygen that a body is capable of utilizing during a workout.

VOLUME: In weight training, refers to the total number of sets and repetitions completed in a single workout.

VOLUME TRAINING: A method of weight training that uses a high number of total sets and repetitions in a single workout.

WARM-UP: The act of gradually increasing intensity during a workout performed to slowly raise the rate of the heart and prepare the body for upcoming activity.

WORKOUT: Refers to the total time that a person spends exercising or the total exercise routine.

WORKING IN: Refers to working with another trainee on gym equipment.

YOGA: In fitness, an exercise associated with the practice of postures.

Index

A

Accountant 215, 226
Advertise 131, 134
Advice 15, 20, 104, 130, 159, 226
Aerobics 15, 138, 175, 218
Attorney 151, 155, 210, 217, 219, 233

B

Body 14, 15, 21, 92, 99, 110, 122, 123,
    127, 130, 170, 171, 190, 198,
    216, 217, 238
Broker 222
Business 15, 16, 20, 21, 86-89, 94-97,
    99, 101-105, 107, 108, 111, 113,
    115, 116, 118-127, 129, 132,
    133, 135-139, 141-160, 162-176,
    178, 179, 181-184, 186-189, 191,
    194-207, 210-217, 219-228, 230,
    231, 233-236

C

Cardio 15
Client 99, 103, 108, 118-120, 122-124,
    126, 127, 143, 161, 169, 170,
    191-193, 197, 210, 218, 219, 230,
    232-237

Club 17, 223
Competition 20, 87, 103, 113, 115-117,
    123, 125, 126, 142, 161, 162,
    165, 168, 188, 193, 198, 199, 213
Credibility 136, 210
Credit 149, 152, 187, 210, 229, 235, 236

D

Design 128
Develop 99, 206
Diet 21

E

Economy 20, 118, 225
Employee 86, 95, 102, 103, 158, 201,
    204, 206, 223, 231-233
Enjoy 97, 147, 151, 192
Equipment 20, 86, 102, 104, 106, 116,
    118, 119, 129, 206, 213, 220, 225
Evaluate 162, 164
Exercise 14, 16, 17, 19, 20, 21, 94,
    96-98, 106, 119, 120, 126, 130,
    140, 221, 230
Expert 15, 20, 96, 99, 182

F

Feedback 20, 92, 120, 145, 172, 222

Fiscal 201, 202
Fitness 15, 16, 19, 20, 21, 94, 99, 105,
    108, 111, 115, 117, 118, 121, 124,
    126, 127, 130, 144, 166, 170,
    171, 172, 174, 176, 188, 204,
    221, 222, 233

G

Growth 22, 94, 105
Gym 17, 21, 103, 119, 122, 124, 126,
    129, 176, 182, 194, 198, 199, 220

H

Health 98, 102, 106, 107, 109, 115, 117,
    118, 119, 122, 127, 128, 132, 142,
    171, 172, 176, 191, 200, 221
Home 91, 92, 105, 119, 121, 122, 129,
    134, 136, 147, 173, 200, 226, 227

I

Incentive 112
Independent 102, 154, 179, 199, 206,
    207, 208, 231, 232

J

Job 87, 88, 94, 95, 103, 124, 136, 173,
    177, 180, 188, 199, 209, 211, 215,
    224, 226, 231, 232

L

Labor 20, 89, 179, 208, 231, 233
Law 98, 153, 157, 158, 224
Leisure 16, 134
Level 16, 20, 85, 86, 87, 88, 95, 96, 97,
    98, 99, 108, 130, 136, 159, 170,
    217, 220, 221, 222
Life style 20, 170

M

Marketing 89, 102, 108, 112-115, 120,
    121, 125-127, 129, 142, 144, 170,
    175, 196, 197
Movement 92

Muscle 22, 131, 218

O

Operate 14, 15, 21, 103, 105, 125, 142,
    159, 182, 217

P

Personal Trainer 14, 15, 85, 86, 88,
    89, 91, 93-96, 98, 99, 101, 103,
    107-109, 111, 112, 115-117,
    119-123, 127, 132, 136, 139, 142,
    163, 166-168, 173-175, 186-188,
    200, 206, 220-222, 227
Protein 15, 220

R

Record 157, 161, 225, 227, 228, 229
Relax 144

S

Schedule 125, 135, 176, 201
Statistics 20, 115
Strength 16, 19, 21, 104
Style 20, 129, 135, 170

T

Teach 15, 21, 105
Time 15, 19, 20, 87-91, 93, 95, 99, 102,
    103, 105, 106, 108-110, 112, 113,
    119, 120, 122-124, 128, 130, 134,
    135, 137, 141, 144, 145, 171-177,
    179, 181, 184, 188, 191-193, 199,
    203, 204, 210, 212, 213, 218,
    222, 226-228, 233, 236
Train 87, 216, 224, 237

V

Variety 20, 96, 143, 197

W

Web site 107, 131-135, 171, 202, 219,
    232
Workout 109, 119, 122, 230